From the library of

Eugénie Muddle

Salute to the
SOLDIER POETS

When you go home
Tell them of us and say
For your tomorrow
We gave our today

Inscribed on the memorial to the 2nd Infantry Division at Kohima Cemetery, near the border between Burma and India. It was at Kohima in 1944 that British troops defeated the Japanese army, bringing a halt to their relentless advance across Asia.

Salute to the
SOLDIER POETS

This England

First published in 1990
by This England Books,
73 Rodney Road, Cheltenham, Gloucestershire

Printed in Great Britain by

BPCC Wheatons Ltd, Exeter

ISBN 0 906324 14 9

CONTENTS

FOREWORD

Although many outstanding and enduring works of literature have been written by men and women who enjoyed seemingly quiet, unremarkable existences, it often takes a traumatic event in a writer's life to ignite the spark of genius within him. This is particularly true when writing verse, for you only have to open a collection of English poetry to discover the power that emotional experiences such as love, death and personal suffering have had in inspiring our greatest poets.

One of the most shattering experiences to which any person can be exposed is war, and in terms of geographical scale, horror and the numbers of people killed, the two great conflicts of the 20th century were without precedent or parallel. During the First World

War hundreds of thousands of brave, idealistic young men found themselves fighting and dying in conditions so appalling that it must have seemed to them as if they had entered Hell itself. Unlike previous wars, many of the ordinary soldiers who had to endure the muddy, rat-infested trenches and nightmarish landscapes of barbed wire and shell craters were well-educated men with backgrounds in the various professions. Before the war some had even been burgeoning poets, and so it isn't surprising that during the long intervals between action they should have found solace by continuing to put their thoughts and feelings down on paper.

What is remarkable, however, is the tremendous emotional intensity that they brought to their work — proof again, if any were needed, of the terrible torment and turmoil that they were all going through. Where once their words had spoken softly, in gentle, predictable rhythms, now they blazed white-hot with energy and urgency, possessed with the power to disturb and shock at one moment, to move to tears the next.

The moods of the poems were as varied as the men. In the early days of the war there were patriotic pieces like Rupert Brooke's famous *The Soldier*. Later on, disillusionment took over, leading to stinging criticism of the military hierarchy and anger at the needless slaughter of so many young men. This outrage found expression in the bitter sarcasm of Siegfried Sassoon's poetry and in the horrifying descriptions of conditions at the Front which were such a stark and disturbing feature of Wilfred Owen's work. A recurring theme in a great number of the poems, and one which was brought on by the soldiers being such a long way from their homes and loved ones, was the way in which the ordinary, everyday things of life assumed a desperate importance. For Edward Thomas these "everyday things" were the meadows, woods and leafy lanes of rural England, and he described these in poems which are, at times, almost painful in their beauty and simplicity.

Whatever the mood or the message, all the poems were created out of the knowledge that death could occur at any moment and the burning need, kindled by compassion for the ordinary footslogger, to tell people back home the truth about how their menfolk were living and dying in the trenches, and to honour and remember all their compatriots who had sacrificed their lives.

Much the same can be said about the poetry of the Second World War, even if it doesn't excite quite the same emotional response as the verses written by the men on the Somme. Nevertheless, there were soldiers, sailors and airmen who wrote with rare power and perception, and even though limitations on space mean that we have tended in this book to concentrate on the poetry of the Great War, Second World War poetry will continue to be featured in *This England*'s "Salute the Soldier Poets" series, from which all these chapters are taken.

Some of the finest poems, from both world wars, remain virtually the only examples of a poet's work — for there were many young men who were tragically cut down before their full genius had had time to flower. Then there are other pieces of verse, which were discovered from time to time scribbled on the backs of old envelopes and empty cigarette packets, for whom there is no known author. But whoever the poets, whether famous or unknown, critically acclaimed or not, just by reading their poetry and learning about the wars that inspired them we are remembering not only those gifted young men, but every soldier, sailor and airman who fought and often died in defence of our country so that we could live in freedom. As the poet Laurence Binyon wrote in 1914, in a poignant poem that has become synonymous with remembering the fallen of the two world wars:

They shall not grow old, as we that are left grow old:
Age shall not weary them, nor the years condemn.
At the going down of the sun and in the morning
We will remember them.

We are trying to do just that in this book, not only for those who have shared the experience of losing loved ones in conflict, but for the young of this generation who hopefully will never know the carnage of another world war.

STEPHEN GARNETT

C·C·

Rupert Brooke in 1913. During the early days of the First World War he was the most celebrated soldier-poet.

RUPERT BROOKE

(1887-1915)

Rupert Chawner Brooke was born at Rugby, in Warwickshire, just over a century ago, on 3rd August 1887, the second of three brothers. His father was a master at Rugby School and Rupert became a pupil there when he was 14, having previously been a day boy at nearby Hillbrow. They were happy schooldays, with Rupert winning various poetry prizes and also distinguishing himself at rugger and cricket.

In 1906 he won a classical scholarship to King's College, Cambridge, where he entered into all aspects of student life. A tall, handsome figure, whose company was sought by everyone, he became President of the University Fabian Society and helped to found the Marlowe Dramatic Society, acting in a number of productions himself. Unfortunately Rupert's hectic social life — which included a number of romantic attachments — took its toll on his studies and he was terribly disappointed to get only a second in his classical tripos in May 1909. For his fourth year he decided to change from Classics to English and also to move out of college with its many distractions and take lodgings in the picturesque village of Grantchester — first in a house known as "The Orchard", then in the "Old Vicarage" with its large garden leading down to the River Granta.

Rupert Brooke working in the garden of the Old Vicarage, Grantchester.

The picnics and boating parties continued, but Rupert applied himself to his work, winning the Harness Essay Prize with a piece entitled *Puritanism in the Early Drama* (1910) and studying the Elizabethan dramatist John Webster in the hope of winning a Fellowship at King's. His life at Cambridge was varied by visits to London, Munich and Berlin, and, following the death of his father in 1910, by a term at Rugby during which he acted as a temporary housemaster.

Rupert had been writing poetry throughout his career at Cambridge and in December 1911 he published, at his own expense, a volume of *Poems*. Many critics were shocked by the poems' unromantic realism, but few could fail to be impressed by the promise they showed. He followed this success by gaining his Fellowship in 1912 and in the same year, writing a one-act play *Lithuania*.

At this point in his life, while he was working on new poems, giving lectures and writing reviews, Rupert was becoming increasingly drawn into a large and interesting circle of literary men and women. Among these were Edward Marsh, John Masefield (whose long narrative poem *The Everlasting Mercy* had just been published and was setting English poetry off in a new direction), James Elroy Flecker and Walter de la Mare. He was also friendly with the family of Winston Churchill, then First Lord of the Admiralty.

Edward Marsh was planning a book called *Georgian Poetry* to celebrate the "new strength and beauty of English verse" and invited Rupert to contribute. This Rupert did, with five poems, but he also helped to edit and energetically publicise the work. *Georgian Poetry 1911-12*, whose other contributors included W.H. Davies, John Drinkwater, Walter de la Mare and D.H. Lawrence, was a very important book in the development of English poetry and the reaction of the public to its appearance shocked even the most optimistic of their number. Demand for it was such that it had to be constantly reprinted and was eventually joined by two further volumes.

In May 1913 Rupert set out on a year of travel to America, Canada and the South Seas, a journey that proved what a great talent he had as a travel writer. He departed from Liverpool and there is a touching story that as there was no-one to see him off, feeling rather lonely Rupert gave sixpence to a little boy called William and asked him to wave to him from the quayside. The boy earned his money, even shouting messages of farewell. "The last object I looked at," wrote the poet,

The Old Vicarage, Grantchester

An excerpt from the full poem written in Berlin, May 1912.

By Rupert Brooke

God! I will pack, and take a train,
And get me to England once again!
For England's the one land, I know,
Where men with Splendid Hearts may go;
And Cambridgeshire, of all England,
The shire for Men who Understand;
And of *that* district I prefer
The lovely hamlet Grantchester.

For Cambridge people rarely smile,
Being urban, squat, and packed with guile;
And Royston men in the far South
Are black and fierce and strange of mouth;
At Over they fling oaths at one,
And worse than oaths at Trumpington,
And Ditton girls are mean and dirty,
And there's none in Harston under thirty,
And folks in Shelford and those parts
Have twisted lips and twisted hearts,
And Barton men make Cockney rhymes,
And Coton's full of nameless crimes,
And things are done you'd not believe
At Madingley, on Christmas Eve.
Strong men have run for miles and miles,
When one from Cherry Hinton smiles;
Strong men have blanched,
                      and shot their wives,
Rather than send them to St. Ives;
Strong men have cried like babes, bydam,
To hear what happened at Babraham.
But Grantchester! ah, Grantchester!
There's peace and holy quiet there,
Great clouds along pacific skies,
And men and women with straight eyes,
Lithe children lovelier than a dream,
A bosky wood, a slumbrous stream,

And little kindly winds that creep
Round twilight corners, half asleep.
In Grantchester their skins are white;
They bathe by day, they bathe by night;
The women there do all they ought;
The men observe the Rules of Thought.
They love the Good; they worship Truth;
They laugh uproariously in youth;
(And when they get to feeling old,
They up and shoot themselves, I'm told) . . .

Ah God! to see the branches stir
Across the moon at Grantchester!
To smell the thrilling-sweet and rotten
Unforgettable, unforgotten
River-smell, and hear the breeze
Sobbing in the little trees.
Say, do the elm-clumps greatly stand,
Still guardians of that holy land?
The chestnuts shade, in reverend dream,
The yet unacademic stream?
Is dawn a secret shy and cold
Anadyomene, silver-gold?
And sunset still a golden sea
From Haslingfield to Madingley?
And after, ere the night is born,
Do hares come out about the corn?

Oh, is the water sweet and cool,
Gentle and brown, above the pool?
And laughs the immortal river still
Under the mill, under the mill?
Say, is there Beauty yet to find?
And Certainty? and Quiet kind?
Deep meadows yet, for to forget
The lies, and truths, and pain? ... oh! yet
Stands the Church clock at ten to three?
And is there honey still for tea?

◁Lascelles Abercrombie, who encouraged Rupert to continue writing.

(Continued from page 13)

"was a small dot waving a white handkerchief (or nearly white) faithfully."

It was a very enjoyable and hugely informative trip, commemorated in sparkling prose in the 13 articles that were published subsequently in the *Westminster Gazette*. He also sent home several poems for inclusion in *New Numbers*, a poetry magazine that two of the "Georgian" poets, Lascelles Abercrombie and Wilfred Gibson, were producing near Dymock, in Gloucestershire.

Rupert returned to England in June 1914, resuming old friendships with the Asquiths and Churchills and enjoying a busy social life of luncheons and theatrical parties. He impressed everyone he met, his charm and unaffected manner attracting many famous and influential figures. Siegfried Sassoon was one who fell

One of the very first recruitment posters. Appeals such as this persuaded many thousands of young men to enlist.

Rupert (standing, second from left) with members of his battalion.

under his spell and many years later he recalled his first meeting with the recently returned adventurer:

> I was in the presence of one on whom had been conferred all the invisible attributes of a poet. To this his radiant good looks seemed subsidiary. Here, I might

well have thought — had my divinations been expressible — was a being singled out for some transplendent performance, some enshrined achievement.

When war was declared, Rupert gained a commission in a newly-created unit called the Royal Naval Division. His attitude towards the war was at first ambivalent, but after taking part in the Antwerp expedition (October 1914) and witnessing the terrible suffering of the thousands of refugees, he became intensely patriotic and anti-German. The attempt to relieve Antwerp failed and Rupert was soon back in London, telling the tale of their expedition to Winston Churchill in person.

On 28th February 1915, after a period of leave in which he wrote his famous war sonnets (they appeared in the last issue of *New Numbers*), Rupert and his division sailed for the Dardanelles with the intention of defeating the Turks and linking up with the Russians. He was terribly excited about the prospect of action, seeing it as a sort of romantic crusade.

Rupert and his men were based on the Greek island of Lemnos, but shortly after taking part in a feint attack when they were ordered back from a major landing at the last moment, they were moved to Skyros, a place of breathtaking beauty and peace. It was here that Rupert received a letter from Edward Marsh telling him that on Easter Sunday the Dean of St. Paul's had read his poem "The Soldier" as part of his sermon and praised its author as "a young writer who would take rank with our great poets". The issue of *New Numbers* in which the poem appeared sold out immediately.

On 20th April, Rupert took part in a Divisional Field Day, but the next morning he was suddenly taken ill. His condition worsened and acute blood poisoning was diagnosed. His friends carried him to a French hospital ship, but there was nothing that the doctors could do and on St. George's Day 1915 he quietly and painlessly passed away. He was buried in a lovely olive grove on Skyros, where the air was heavy with the scent of flowering sage. On his wooden cross the following words were written:

HERE LIES
THE SERVANT OF GOD
SUB-LIEUTENANT IN THE
ENGLISH NAVY
WHO DIED FOR
THE DELIVERANCE OF
CONSTANTINOPLE FROM
THE TURKS

He had left a note saying that any royalties from his poems were to be shared among Wilfred Gibson, Lascelles Abercrombie and Walter de la Mare "to help them write good stuff, instead of me". It was a thoughtful gesture and one which, bearing in mind the immense popularity of Brooke's poems immediately after his death, proved to be of great help for the three men concerned. At a time when patriotism and belief in the heroism of the war were at their height, Brooke's "Soldier" seemed to put into words what the vast majority of English people thought and felt. Later poets, exposed to the horrors of the trenches, would ruthlessly puncture this attitude, but at the time Rupert Brooke became something of an idealised, romantic hero. It is interesting to wonder what course his poetry would have taken had he lived longer. He had shown such great promise in poems like "The Old Vicarage, Grantchester" and one cannot help echoing the age-old cry: "What might have been . . ?"

STEPHEN GARNETT

The poet's grave on Skyros in 1915.

The Soldier

If I should die, think only this of me:
That there's some corner of a foreign field
That is for ever England. There shall be
In that rich earth a richer dust concealed;
A dust whom England bore, shaped, made aware,
Gave, once, her flowers to love, her ways to roam,
A body of England's, breathing English air,
Washed by the rivers, blest by suns of home.

And think, this heart, all evil shed away,
A pulse in the eternal mind, no less
Gives somewhere back the thoughts by England given;
Her sights and sounds; dreams happy as her day;
And laughter, learnt of friends; and gentleness,
In hearts at peace, under an English heaven.

RUPERT BROOKE

Siegfried Sassoon in 1915, aged 29.

SIEGFRIED SASSOON

(1886-1967)

I t was the end of June 1916 on the battle-scarred Western Front in France. Sheltering in a deep trench, the men of the 1st Battalion, The Royal Welch Fusiliers, were patiently awaiting the order that would send them "over the top" towards their next objective — a strongly-defended copse that had been unsuccessfully attacked on the previous day. Not expecting any decisive movement for a while, few of the weary soldiers saw the lone, khaki-clad figure who climbed out of the trench and set off on a solitary run towards the German positions. A couple of rifles gave him covering fire, but he charged so swiftly that very soon he had disappeared from sight. A German machine gun rattled, a bomb exploded, and an uneasy silence settled once more on the scene . . .

But that courageous soldier had not, as those who saw him might have assumed, been killed during his reckless attack. Shouting and throwing bombs like a madman he had literally frightened the Germans away and taken the trench single-handed! Once there, he did a curious thing. Rather than backing up his heroic action by calling for reinforcements, he made himself comfortable in the corner of the trench, took a book of poetry from out of his pocket and proceeded to read it.

The picturesque Weald of Kent, where Siegfried Sassoon was born. He loved to ramble by himself, studying nature.

The soldier's name was Siegfried Sassoon, the celebrated First World War poet, and his attack on that German position was typical of numerous other actions he had performed: a combination of bravery, foolhardiness and a general couldn't-care-less attitude which was fuelled by his growing anger at the futility and waste of war.

This dashing dare-devilry earned him the nickname of "Mad Jack" by his companions, but it is the powerful poems written in between these bursts of fighting for which he is remembered today.

Siegfried Loraine Sassoon was born on 8th September, 1886 at "Weirleigh", a rambling Victorian house on the outskirts of Brenchley in a beautiful part of the Weald of Kent. Alfred and Theresa Sassoon had two other sons — Michael, born in 1884, and Hamo, born in 1887 — but it was for Siegfried that a particularly strong bond was formed, especially between mother and son.

Although he suffered one great sorrow when he was only eight years old, with the separation of his parents and subsequent early death of his father from tuberculosis, Siegfried's childhood was very happy and he was devoted to his mother. Theresa Sassoon was an artist and sculptor, a vivacious, forthright and original character who firmly believed that one day Siegfried would become a great poet. She encouraged his early attempts at verse, passed on to him her enthusiasm for riding and hunting, and nurtured within him a love of Nature and the countryside.

Siegfried was something of a loner, becoming used to his own company during periods of childhood illness when he was carried out to the garden to read and daydream alone with the sights and sounds of Nature. He loved to listen to the white pigeons cooing on the

Marlborough College today. Siegfried enjoyed rugby here and learned to play the organ.

high-tiled roof, the squawking of jays down among the peas and the horses stamping in the stable yard. So while his brothers were occupied in typical boyish pursuits he preferred quieter more contemplative occupations: fishing in the pond in the orchard or exploring the stream for a moorhen's nest. While Michael and Hamo were engaged in engineering experiments in the workshop, Siegfried would be busy copying out poems for his mother on a toy printing press. He loved listening to music, enjoyed playing the piano himself, and from an early age had a passion for cricket. Michael and Hamo were usually too busy to play with him but Richardson, the groom, was always willing to bowl to him in the stable yard.

As their mother thought they were delicate the Sassoon boys did not go to school until they were in their teens, and received their education from various tutors. Books were very important to Siegfried. Besides reading the many volumes which the family library contained, especially the poets Longfellow, Shelley and Tennyson ("The Lady of Shalott" was his favourite), he sent away for historical romances by Stanley Weyman, which were delivered by carrier's cart from nearby Paddock Wood station every Saturday afternoon.

Eventually, Theresa Sassoon conceded the necessity of sending the boys to school in spite of her fears regarding such supposed health hazards as the drains and the feeding arrangements. A prep school at Sevenoaks was chosen. Michael went there first and Siegfried followed in 1900. He liked school, did well at cricket and, more importantly, was able to catch up on his academic work. The excellent coaching at Sevenoaks enabled him, in 1902, to pass the entrance examination to Marlborough. His public school career

was not, however, much of a success, for he was dogged by ill-health. He nearly died of complications related
to an attack of measles and this was followed by a strain-
ed heart caused by trying too hard at rugger, and oph-
thalmia in both eyes through an excess of book work.
On the credit side he played for his house eleven,

Clare College, Cambridge, where Sassoon read Law.

learned the organ and wrote a few occasional poems.

In October 1905 Siegfried went up to Clare College, Cambridge, where he led a life of blissful indolence, playing golf, writing poetry on random subjects and only spasmodically reading Law. Manifestly unsuited to tackle a subject which offered no scope for the imagination, he eventually left Cambridge without taking a degree and after having a volume of his poems printed privately he decided to devote himself to becoming a poet. Disappointingly, he did not achieve instant recognition. The poems of this period lacked interest because he had nothing much to write about. The treatment was too unnatural and the verbal imagery too remote from personal observation.

During the next few years Siegfried settled at "Weirleigh" with his mother, leading the life of a country gentleman. When poetry temporarily deserted him, besides cricket and golf, fox-hunting provided a welcome diversion. His *Memoirs of a Fox-Hunting Man* which was published in 1928 reveals his passion for the sport. Siegfried relates his exploits in the hunting field with modest irony, describing many embarrassing moments, but he was actually a first-class performer, winning several point-to-point races on his lovely bay horse "Cockbird" and once carrying off the Colonel's Cup.

After a while, he decided that if his poetry were to succeed he must move in intellectual circles. His mother's friend, Edmund Gosse, critic and man of letters, had already given him some encouragement and now Edward Marsh the compiler of *Georgian Poetry* suggested that he should take a flat in London from where he could mingle in literary society.

By the summer of 1914 his sojourn in the metropolis had brought the would-be poet no tangible results and he was considerably in debt. The outbreak of the Great War solved his problem. He enlisted as a trooper in the Sussex Yeomanry, and in 1915 was commissioned in The Royal Welch Fusiliers and posted to France. Shortly before he went overseas in November 1915,

The Hero

'Jack fell as he'd have wished,' the Mother said,
And folded up the letter that she'd read.
'The Colonel writes so nicely.' Something broke
In the tired voice that quavered to a choke.
She half looked up. 'We mothers are so proud
Of our dead soldiers.' Then her face was bowed.

Quietly the Brother Officer went out.
He'd told the poor old dear some gallant lies
That she would nourish all her days, no doubt.
For while he coughed and mumbled, her weak eyes
Had shone with gentle triumph, brimmed with joy,
Because he'd been so brave, her glorious boy.

He thought how 'Jack', cold-footed, useless swine,
Had panicked down the trench that night the mine
Went up at Wicked Corner; how he'd tried
To get sent home, and how, at last, he died,
Blown to small bits. And no one seemed to care
Except that lonely woman with white hair.

SIEGFRIED SASSOON

33

Siegfried received news of the death in France of one of his best friends from hunting days. It hurt him deeply and when soon afterwards he heard that his brother Hamo had died of wounds in the Gallipoli campaign, his attitude to the war began to change. Up to that point he had shared the accepted view that it was noble to fight and die in the trenches, but when he experienced the terrible conditions and suffering endured by most soldiers he felt an urgent need to dispel war's romantic illusions. The intensity of his feelings fanned the poetic spark within him into flames, and at last he was writing of genuinely felt experiences. The war had turned him into a poet, as the following lines *To My Brother* demonstrate:

Give me your hand, my brother, search my face;
Look into these eyes lest I should think of shame;
For we have made an end of all things base.
We are returning by the road we came.

Your lot is with the ghosts of soldiers dead,
And I am in the field where men must fight.
But in the gloom I see your laurell'd head
And through your victory I shall win the light.

He sustained another personal loss in the death of his dear friend and fellow officer David Thomas, the "Tommy" of his poems. These several deaths spurred Siegfried on to deeds of valour in revenge for what they had suffered. He regarded such exploits, which sometimes amounted to foolhardiness, as being no more laudable than his old ambition to win a steeplechase. He did, however, win the Military Cross for remaining for 90 minutes under rifle and bomb fire collecting and bringing in the wounded. When not in

Siegfried Sassoon on leave in 1916.

action, Siegfried became deeply concerned about his men, distressed that GHQ seemed to treat them as little more than cannon fodder.

When he was invalided home with trench fever in 1916, he found himself resenting the attitude of civilians and more particularly of those leaders who spoke of the war as heroic. He increasingly turned to poetry to express his feelings; bitter and satirical poems which were "deliberately written to disturb complacency".

On 16th April, 1917 Siegfried Sassoon was wounded in France — hit in the shoulder while leading a party of bombers up to the Hindenburg line. His sick leave in England coincided with the publication of his first volume of war poetry, *The Old Huntsman*. Many of the poems revealed his revulsion at the apparent indifference on the part of the War Office to the colossal waste of human life. While he convalesced his mind was oppressed by the thought of the men of his regiment constantly under fire. At the same time he felt guilty at enjoying a respite from the action and being able to relax with books and music and the comforts of home, especially when he saw other officers leading safe lives far away from the fighting. Again, his anger was poured out in stark verse:

If I were fierce, and bald, and short of breath,
I'd live with scarlet Majors at the Base,
And speed glum heroes up the line to death.
You'd see me with my puffy petulant face,
Guzzling and gulping in the best hotel,
Reading the Roll of Honour. "Poor young chap,"
I'd say, — "I used to know his father well;
Yes, we've lost heavily in this last scrap."
And when the war is done and youth stone dead,
I'd toddle safely home and die — in bed.

Siegfried's friends tried to persuade him to take a job at home, but though he was suffering from frayed nerves, depression and occasional hallucinations, he felt that even if he did not return to the Front he must become the spokesman of the common soldier and inform the War Office what they surely did not wish to hear, that the war he had entered as a war of defence and liberation had now become one of aggression and conquest. He sent a statement to this effect to his Commanding Officer, declaring his action to be one of wilful defiance of military authority. To underline his protest, while awaiting a medical board at Litherland Camp, he threw his MC ribbon into the River Mersey! Thanks to the influence of his friend, fellow poet and soldier, Robert Graves, Siegfried was not court-martialled but declared to be mentally disturbed as a result of shell-shock and drafted to a military hospital in Edinburgh. Here he was treated by the psychologist W.H. Rivers, for whom he developed a great liking and respect. He also made friends with one of the other patients, the poet Wilfred Owen. The two met when Owen, who was a great admirer of Sassoon's work, appeared in his room with several copies of *The Old Huntsman* which he asked Siegfried to autograph. He then, rather nervously, showed Siegfried some of his own poems. Siegfried was full of admiration and a firm friendship developed between them. The death of Owen in November 1918, only a week before the Armistice, was a further shattering blow to Sassoon.

The General

'Good-morning; good-morning!' the General said
When we met him last week on our way to the line.
Now the soldiers he smiled at are most of 'em dead,
And we're cursing his staff for incompetent swine.
'He's a cheery old card,' grunted Harry to Jack
As they slogged up to Arras with rifle and pack.

But he did for them both by his plan of attack.

SIEGFRIED SASSOON

Robert Graves, a friend and fellow poet who helped save Siegfried from a court martial.

No-one really believed Sassoon was mentally unstable. His war poems were sufficient proof to the contrary, but in order to confirm it he decided in November 1917 to apply for active service again in the hope that he might be drafted back into his old regiment. Siegfried's sanity was vindicated and he was sent overseas with the 25th Battalion of The Royal Welch Fusiliers, first to Palestine and in May 1918 back to France. The following month the second volume of his war poems *Counter-Attack* was published.

Back in the familiar surroundings of the trenches, Siegfried tried to prove his solidarity with his men by becoming involved in dangerous escapades. In July 1918 he made a foray into No-Man's-Land, as a result of which he was wounded in the head and invalided home for the last time. Siegfried felt frustrated that his military career had come to such an inglorious end. Despite the fact that back in London he found himself lionised as a soldier-poet and met interesting literary figures like Masefield, Drinkwater and T.E. Lawrence, the old carefree life of hunting, cricket and writing poetry no longer appealed. He dabbled in politics and in March 1919 became literary editor of the socialist *Daily Herald*, a post which gave him an introduction to contemporary poets like Edmund Blunden who became a life-long friend.

At the beginning of 1920 Siegfried undertook a highly successful tour of the United States, but back in England — like so many of his generation in the immediate post-war period — he felt restless and disillusioned. He still wanted to be a poet and also to write prose, but the war had been his inspiration and now he lacked incentive. From 1920 Siegfried was based at a friend's flat in London. From here he spent time visiting people of literary and artistic tastes such as the Morrells at Garsington, the Sitwells, David Cecil and H.G. Wells. In an effort to forget the war and what he now considered his foolish protest, he plunged into a round of theatres, concerts and parties interspersed with an occasional sortie into the country for a day with the Hunt. By 1928 he was longing to

◁A portrait of Sassoon in 1920.

return to the country and decided to buy a little manor in good hunting country — "Heytesbury House" in Wiltshire. He had also published his first prose work *The Memoirs of a Fox-Hunting Man.* For this he received the Hawthornden Prize. Its sequel, *Memoirs of an Infantry Officer*, appeared in 1930 and *Sherston's Progress* continued the story in 1936. These three were subsequently published in one volume as *The Complete Memoirs of George Sherston* (1937). On the eve of the outbreak of the Second World War Sassoon published the first of three autobiographical volumes, *The Old Century and Seven More Years* (1938), a nostalgic reconstruction of his childhood and youth to be continued in 1942 by *The Weald of Youth* and the third volume *Siegfried's Journey* (1945). In 1933 Siegfried had married Hester Gatty and in 1936 their son, George, was born.

In The Pink

So Davies wrote: "This leaves me in the pink."
Then scrawled his name: "Your loving sweet-
    heart, Willie."
With crosses for a hug. He'd had a drink
Of rum and tea; and, though the barn was chilly,
For once his blood ran warm; he had pay to spend.
Winter was passing; soon the year would mend.

But he couldn't sleep that night; stiff in the dark
He groaned and thought of Sundays at the farm,
And how he'd go as cheerful as a lark
In his best suit, to wander arm in arm
With brown-eyed Gwen, and whisper in her ear
The simple, silly things she liked to hear.

And, then he thought: tomorrow night we trudge
Up to the trenches, and my boots are rotten.
Five miles of stodgy clay and freezing sludge,
And everything but wretchedness forgotten.
To-night he's in the pink; but soon he'll die.
And still the war goes on — he don't know why.

SIEGFRIED SASSOON

10th February 1916

Heytesbury House in Wiltshire, which the poet bought in 1928 in order to return to the English countryside.

During the Thirties Sassoon's popularity began to fade. Having buried himself in the country he no longer moved in literary and social circles, though his war poems continued to be in demand for anthologies. During the period of the Second World War all that he produced were 33 poems of *Rhymed Ruminations*. After the war he began to write again, trying to philosophise in verse his growing interest in the meaning of life and Man's final destiny. They were published in 1956 under the title *Sequences*, though their appeal was mainly to those of a religious turn of mind.

One of Siegfried's closest friends, whom he had known since 1915, was Sidney Cockerell, a Catholic and a great admirer of Sassoon's poetry. Cockerell happened to send a copy of *Siegfried's Journey* to a nun of the Stanbrook Community in Worcestershire, Dame Felicitas Corrigan. A correspondence developed between the nun and the poet, resulting in Siegfried visiting various religious houses of the Order. As his understanding of the Catholic faith grew, through contact with those who practised it, he began to feel that only in that Church would he find the answer to all his questionings. On the eve of the Assumption, 15th August 1957, at the age of 70, Siegfried was received into the Roman Catholic Church at Downside Abbey, where he had already been a frequent visitor.

During the last decade of his life he became more contemplative and withdrawn from public life. He remained in communication with his old friends such as Edmund Blunden and Sidney Cockerell, made occasional visits to London and up to the age of 74 played cricket at Downside. He was concerned to share his recently acquired spiritual wealth with others through his poems, and he was often asked to read

Downside Abbey, Somerset. Siegfried was received into the Roman Catholic faith here in 1957.

them at religious gatherings. Although his delivery was somewhat halting, through nervousness, his enthusiasm and sincerity made the poems come alive. In 1960 Stanbrook Abbey published a book of Siegfried's religious poems called *The Path to Peace*. It was not well received by the critics who condemned the contents on technical grounds and could not appreciate their sincerity and simplicity of expression.

During the last two years of his life his health began to fail, but this enforced inactivity did provide him with more time for spiritual reading, music and for the writing and receiving of letters. He rejoiced at the election of his old friend Edmund Blunden to the Chair of Poetry at Oxford, and a letter received from a stranger telling of his conversion after reading the volume of eight of his poems called *The Octave* made him very happy. The poems were issued by the Arts Council to celebrate Siegfried's 80th birthday, and containing as they do the essence of his simple and deeply-held faith, meant more to Siegfried than all his other literary achievements. He no longer desired to be an acclaimed celebrity, but merely a common-sense Christian. Although at the end of his life his physical strength was failing, spiritually he was very much alive and perfectly at peace.

> *Falling asleep . . . the herons, and the hounds . . .*
> *September in the darkness; and the world*
> *I've known; all fading past me into peace.*
> ("Falling Asleep", 1919)

Siegfried fell asleep on 1st September, 1967, a week before his 81st birthday, and was buried in the churchyard at Mells in Somerset.

ELIZABETH SAINTSBURY

*A soldier in North Africa in 1942 writes
a letter home.*

Stay With Me, God

This moving prayer-poem is anonymous, for the scrap
of paper on which it was written fluttered into the hands of
a British soldier sheltering in a slit trench in North Africa
during the last war. Where it came from, or who wrote it,
no-one knows. But its sentiment and truth will be readily
recognised by Servicemen of both wars who faced untold
fears in those terrible years of conflict.

Stay with me, God, the night is dark,
The night is cold: my little spark
Of courage dies. The night is long;
Be with me, God, and make me strong.

I love a game, I love a fight.
I hate the dark; I love the light.
I love my child; I love my wife.
I am no coward, I love Life.

Life with its change of mood and shade.
I want to live. I'm not afraid,
But me and mine are hard to part;
Oh, unknown God, lift up my heart.

You stilled the waters at Dunkirk
And saved your servants. All your work
Is wonderful, Dear God. You strode
Before us down that dreadful road.

We were alone, and hope had fled;
We loved our country and our dead,
And could not shame them; so we stayed
The course, and were not much afraid.

Dear God, that nightmare road! And then
That Sea! We got there . . . we were men.
My eyes were blind, my feet were torn,
My soul sang like a bird at dawn!

I knew that death is but a door.
I knew what we were fighting for:
Peace for the kids, our brothers freed,
A kinder world, a cleaner breed.

I'm but the son my mother bore,
A simple man and nothing more.
But — God of strength and gentleness,
Be pleased to make me nothing less.

Help me, O God, when Death is near
To mock the haggard face of fear,
That when I fall — if fall I must —
My soul may triumph in the Dust.

JAMES FARRAR

(1923-1944)

The summer of 1944 was cold and miserable, with the unseasonal showers and blustery winds causing almost as much comment in cottages and public houses across England as the exciting news from Europe where the armies of Germany were being relentlessly driven back on every front. But if a person in one of those cottage gardens happened suddenly to stop what they were doing, shield their eyes with their hand and peer upwards towards the sky, as things stood in 1944 it was unlikely to be a brief glimpse of that much-missed sun that they were looking for. One of their hands would probably be cupped to their ear, listening intently to a tell-tale buzzing noise like the sound of a distant motor-bike engine. If the buzzing suddenly stopped, to be replaced by an eerie silence, they knew that they had exactly fifteen seconds in which to run for cover before a mighty explosion ripped nearby buildings apart, reducing them to dust and rubble.

This sinister threat from the skies which so preoccupied men, women and children throughout the summer of 1944 was Hitler's last desperate attempt to bring this nation to its knees — by the use of the infamous V-1 flying bomb, or "doodlebug" as it was quickly nicknamed. Hundreds of these frightening

James Farrar at the age of 20.

A remarkable picture of a doodlebug on its final dive over London.

weapons were aimed at London and it became an important task of the RAF either to destroy the factories where they were made, or to intercept them in flight and shoot them down over the sea before they could reach their targets.

One of the many young men involved in these patrols to seek out and destroy the doodlebugs was a 20-year-old aircraft navigator named James Farrar. Night sorties in a Mosquito aircraft over the English Channel had become fairly routine to him, but as he and his pilot took off from an airfield near Cambridge in the early hours of 26th July, 1944, they both had special personal reasons for wanting to stop the flying-bombs

A de Havilland Mosquito, like the one James Farrar used to fly to hunt down doodlebugs.

from reaching England. Only a few days before the flight the pilot's wife and children had had a narrow escape when their house was smashed to pieces by a V-1 and as James's mother lived directly below the regular flight-path of the doodlebugs on their way to London, he had the satisfaction of knowing that every flying-bomb shot down would be one less danger to her.

As dawn was breaking over the icy English Channel a radio message informed them that a V-1 had been spotted in their vicinity and they were to find and destroy it. Their progress was followed on a radar screen back at operational headquarters — a tiny blob of light which flashed, faded slowly, and flashed again. Then, with the Mosquito flying at a height of 7,000 feet and some 25 miles north-east of Margate, the flashing light suddenly disappeared from the screen.

No-one will ever know exactly what happened in those final few moments, but it was assumed afterwards that they had flown too close to their target and collided with it. As might be expected, the sense of loss at such a terrible waste of life was acute, but no-one beyond James Farrar's immediate family realised just how great a loss England and the world of literature had suffered by the death of that particular young man. Had he survived the war he would now, in all probability, be well known both as a novelist and a poet. As it was, his inspiration was only able to find private expression on the pages of a large journal that he kept, recording his personal thoughts and experiences, and sprinkled with short stories and pieces of verse which were remarkably mature for one who was so young.

It was this journal which, after he had read it in 1946, led Henry Williamson the popular country writer and author of *Tarka the Otter* to describe James Farrar as "a poet and prose-writer of the rare first-class . . . an authentic voice of those who fell in the war, and of those who survived". Williamson was so impressed with the entries in the journal that four years later he published it in book form with a title suggested by James's mother, *The Unreturning Spring*.

So who exactly was this bright young man whose life and genius shone as briefly and intensely as the flashing light on that radar screen?

James Farrar was born on 5th October, 1923, at Woodford in Essex, the younger son of a mother and father who separated when he was still a child. Both James and his brother David were intelligent boys and while still a pupil at a school in Sutton, Surrey, James was aware of wanting to be a writer — jotting down page after page of random thoughts, poems and prose essays for a future work "unnamed and unwritten". The boys were brought up by their devoted mother, but they continued to see their father and James must

The Beloved

When I am in the fields she lies
Alone upon the hills, for she is Day
And I am Night, and brightest shine her eyes
When I must look away
But briefly as in summer dawn we meet,
Her beauty in a flood
Burns vagrant through my blood.

And when the swift floats high
On molten tide of sunset, silently
Together in the meadows do we lie,
But never wed shall be:
For soon she sleeps in mist and I must rise,
And when the stars are grown
Must seek the hills alone.

JAMES FARRAR

have heard many tales from Mr. Farrar about his days as a flyer in the Royal Flying Corps during the First World War.

In 1939, when the Second World War broke out, James's school closed down and he worked for several months on a farm at Manaccan in Cornwall. It was an exciting and idyllic time for a young man on the threshold of life and while he was there, happy and carefree, the first passages in what would eventually become *The Unreturning Spring* were written.

Like many gifted writers James was at his happiest when enjoying long solitary walks through the fields and lanes of the English countryside. He was a sharp observer of the world around him and delighted in the local Cornish dialect and the curious place-names which are such a colourful feature of that beautiful corner of England. Sometimes he would tramp all day and into the night, stopping now and then to sniff the heady scent of a wild flower, listen to a snatch of bird-song, or lie on his back in a meadow staring at the stars which shimmered in the heavens high above. He frequently carried with him a pocket-book on wild flowers and was soon acquainted with all the local species, listing them in his diary, as much in love with the sound of their names as with their colours and scents: campion, bitter-sweet and bryony; celandine, speedwell and yellow archangel.

In the spring of 1940 James left Cornwall to return to his mother's house and a temporary job in an accountant's office in London. "I sentence you to death by accountancy", he wrote, with a typical flash of wry humour, and escaped from the mundane world of figures whenever he could, finding solace in the countryside around his home. This was the England of the Battle of Britain and the sights and sounds of war were soon making their mark on many of his favourite haunts. During a trip to the coast in May of that year he heard the faint rumble of guns in France; and then in August he noticed how the noise of anti-aircraft fire had frightened many of the birds away.

Having been a member of the Air Training Corps, he volunteered for the RAF only a few months after his seventeenth birthday, and was at last able to bid a happy farewell to the accountant's office. There followed a series of interviews, examinations and courses, including a stay at Torquay on the Devon coast where he and his fellow cadets had to study from

In 1940, when a German invasion was thought likely, England's beaches were a tangle of barbed wire and barricades.

eight o'clock in the morning until six at night. They also took part in clay-pigeon shooting, physical training on the beach, and on a memorable day in April received their very own flying kits. The note in James's journal which records this momentous event also contained the following passage. It gives a good insight into his thoughts at that time and the happy memories he carried with him:

A letter from mother contained the phrase, "Almond blossom, palm willow, jasmine and daffodils . . . home is full of flowers". Gosh, what I'm going to make up for after the war! That just represents Easter as it should be, and here am I missing it. I like to think of my woods, and all the stages I used to watch — right through to high summer, with such great interest, it seems funny to think of it all going ahead without me, but I feel it has something of my thought in it now. I suppose that's my faith, really. It means that wherever I am there are the same stars and the same living things, all of which are familiar, so that the mere face of the locality is relatively non-important.

James had grown into a tall (6ft. 2in.), easy-going and friendly young man, with broad shoulders, a fresh complexion, brown wavy hair and blue-grey eyes. In many respects some of his experiences were not so very different from those of other ordinary young men of previous and subsequent generations. He enjoyed sports, especially cross-country running, was not above having one or two drinks with his RAF friends, and during his frequent moves around the country began to have his first romantic encounters. But the England in which he grew to manhood, and which he recorded in such faithful detail, has certainly never been the same either before or since. This was an England at war: of mighty Bofors guns beside beaches and barbed wire; of train journeys in draughty corridors crowded with Service men and women; of meetings in Lyons tea-houses and on seats outside village pubs as sweethearts spent a few precious moments of their leave together. It was an England of brief encounters and romances started at crowded dances, with the hope that they might survive the war. And it was an England of men and women who had been injured in the conflict, but who still managed to put on a brave face; and of letters on the doormat which might bring good news, but which could also bring bad . . .

James Farrar was a part of all this, but he also had the writer's unique gift of being able to stand back to observe and comment. He was aware of being rather different from most of his fellows, but watched and questioned himself just as much as he did anybody else.

Beachy Head, Sussex, where James loved to walk in order to think and write.

The course at Torquay was followed in May 1942 by one at Eastbourne in Sussex. When he wasn't studying or taking part in parades he enjoyed rambles and runs to Beachy Head, browsing in bookshops, going to the pictures to see the latest films, and attending, rather nervously, some of the local dances. Even though he was still only 18, James had already hammered out his own philosophy about life and the way in which he intended to live as a writer.

It's quite possible that for a number of years, or even all the time, certain people will not be able to think of me without calling me a failure because I shall not have a house, a car and so on. This does not mean that I intend to ruin my life, because I don't. The picture is this: in an ordinary job I can get a living and even advancement if my youth dies enough for me to raise enthusiam for it, and I shall live like a codfish. If I try my own hand I may or may not get a living, and I shall live alternately like a rainbow-fish and a dolorous deep-sea whale, but I may get a kick out of it.

The next few months were similarly busy, with James moving from one RAF base to another: Bridgnorth (Shropshire), Harrogate (Yorkshire), Staverton (Gloucestershire), Cranfield (Bedfordshire), and in September 1943, Coltishall in Norfolk, by which time he held the rank of Pilot Officer. He entered wholeheartedly into Service life, but still liked to steal away whenever he could to explore the countryside near to the places where he was stationed. He was also a compulsive letter-writer, corresponding with members of his family and several young ladies, and a great admirer of the music of Delius whose moods he tried to capture with his words.

After making his first flight in January 1943, James steadily increased his number of flying hours, anxious to become involved in the "real business" and sensing that it wouldn't be long in coming. When it did come, although he had much less time to devote to his writing, it gave him a wonderful feeling of fulfilment:

God, I shall be sorry when these war days are over, though. I wouldn't have known the first thing about life

but for this marvellous series of ephemeral companion-ships and episodes. And I know I'm getting more guts. In this job above all, because I'm right up against the sights and scenes of this life now.

By the time of that ill-fated final flight he was really enjoying life and was full of plans for the future . . .

Following James's death Mrs. Farrar sent some pieces of her son's work to the editor of *Adelphi,* John Middleton Murry, who published them in his magazine. It was after seeing these that Henry Williamson contacted Mrs. Farrar and began making preparations to publish James's journal. "Had he lived," wrote Williamson in the introduction, "what books James Farrar would have written!"

Sadly, all hope of that came to a sudden end one cold July morning high above the English Channel.

STEPHEN GARNETT

IVOR GURNEY

(1890–1937)

I t was the last day of 1937 and inside the little village
church at Twigworth in Gloucestershire a group
of black-suited mourners were standing in sombre
silence, listening to the old organ as it jerked and
wheezed like a man gasping for his final breath. They
joined in with the words of the song, and as the notes
were carried on the cold winter's air out to the bleak,
bare churchyard where a freshly-dug grave was waiting,
not even the antiquity of the instrument nor their emotional, frequently faltering voices, could destroy the
obvious beauty of the music. Out there, the dark sky,
black-branched trees and rooks flying homeward over
the lonely church, seemed themselves to be dressed for
mourning and lamenting the death of the old year.

But it wasn't the passing of the year that the people
inside the church were mourning. They were gathered
for the funeral of a First World War poet of astonishing
gifts — the man who had also composed the words
and music that they were now bravely attempting to
sing. His name was Ivor Gurney and he died just over
50 years ago, on Boxing Day 1937.

Although there were some among the assembly
who were not acquainted with his tragic story, others
knew only too well the terrible suffering that this tor-
tured genius had endured. He had survived the war,
during which he produced some of the most original

Ivor Gurney wearing his army uniform in 1915.

and unusual poetry of the time, only to suffer a complete mental breakdown which meant that for the last 15 years of his life he had been confined in a number of grim, prison-like institutions.

Looking at the pale faces in the church it was easy to pick out those who had been Ivor's friends. There was the man playing the organ — Herbert Howells, himself a talented musician and composer but whose fingers on that bible-black afternoon felt as heavy as his heart. He missed the golden voice of his dear departed friend; a voice that had once soared like an angel, holding everyone who heard it spellbound. And then there was an elegant elderly lady named Marion Scott. A long-time friend of Ivor and champion of his work, she stood in the congregation sobbing into a lace handkerchief. The man with probably the most memories, though, was Canon Alfred Cheesman who was conducting the funeral service. He could remember Ivor the choir-boy and those happy days just three miles away in Gloucester when the maturing musician and poet had been his prize pupil. By a terrible irony, it was to Cheesman that Mr. and Mrs. David Gurney had brought their son for baptism at the city's All Saints' Church, in September 1890. The memories of that day flickered like dying sparks behind Cheesman's tired eyes. It all seemed so long ago. Who would have thought that dreams so bright could turn into nightmares so dark?

Ivor Bertie Gurney was born on 28th August, 1890, in Queen Street, Gloucester, where his father had a small tailoring business. He was the second of four children. Soon after Ivor's birth the family moved to premises at Barton Street, Gloucester, a dark and dingy house that was not improved by the uneasy, bickering relationship that existed between the parents.

Gloucester Cathedral, where Ivor sang in the choir.

In 1896 Ivor began attending the National School in London Road and also the Sunday school at All Saints', where he immediately fell under the influence of Cheesman who was curate. Encouraged by him, Ivor joined the choir at All Saints' and later secured a place in the Gloucester Cathedral Choir, which meant he automatically became a pupil at the city's King's School, but though he was gaining a reputation as a gifted solo singer, music did not consume his entire

The Gurney family shop in Gloucester.

interests. The surrounding lanes and hills of Gloucestershire began to play an equally important part in his life and soon the picturesque hamlets and villages were as familiar to him as the verses of hymns and psalms. In later years the names of these places would ring like a magical incantation through his poetry . . . Framilode, Maisemore, Redmarley, Cranham . . .

As Ivor's genius and musical ambitions flourished, these rambles became increasingly solitary affairs, a quiet commune between himself and Nature, but at King's School he remained a very normal schoolboy and excelled at both cricket and football. As one of the cities that regularly hosted the great Three Choirs music festival, Gloucester had much to inspire the susceptible young Gurney and by the age of 16 he was determined to become a professional musician. Through regular visits to the home of Alfred Cheesman he also began to appreciate poetry and was introduced to the works of Housman, Kipling, Tennyson and many other poets.

The intellectual world of the curate was a far cry from the commercial atmosphere of his father's tailoring shop, but Ivor's aspirations were greeted with a mixture of pride and suspicion by his parents — pride that he was bettering himself, suspicion that he might be getting ideas above his station. He was gradually growing away from his family and would often disappear for days at a time to explore the Gloucestershire lanes and discuss music and poetry with two other likeminded companions, Herbert Howells and Wilfred Harvey, himself destined to become a poet of some note. Unfortunately, and as a grim portent of what the future held, Ivor's behaviour was becoming increasingly unpredictable. He often went for long periods without food and as well as frequent nights spent sleeping rough in Cotswolds barns or fields, would turn up at friends' houses at all hours of the day or night.

After leaving the Cathedral Choir in 1906, Ivor enrolled as an articled pupil to Dr. Herbert Brewer, the Cathedral organist and a rather conservative instructor who was often exasperated by his independently-minded but very likeable pupil. To help support himself, Ivor also held various organist posts, though because of his outspoken manner none of these lasted very long!

By this time, Ivor had started to write songs seriously and the undoubted merit they displayed convinced Cheesman that his gifted charge should now

seek greater things. The two of them went up to Durham University where Ivor successfully sat the matriculation exam before embarking on a memorable tour of the great cathedral cities of York, Lincoln and Norwich. Spurred on by success Ivor then won an open scholarship to the Royal College of Music and went to London in the autumn of 1911.

At the Royal College, Ivor was known as "Schubert", and another student, Marion Scott, remembered seeing him for the first time and being struck by his unusual appearance in a dark blue river pilot's coat. Marion Scott and Ivor Gurney later became firm friends, and with the arrival at the College of Herbert Howells and a young Australian called

Song of Pain and Beauty

O may these days of pain,
    These wasted-seeming days,
Somewhere reflower again
    With scent and savour of praise.
Draw out of memory all bitterness
    Of night with Thy sun's rays.

And strengthen Thou in me
    The love of men here found,
And eager charity,
    That, out of difficult ground,
Spring like flowers in barren deserts, or
    Like light, or a lovely sound.

A simpler heart than mine
    Might have seen beauty clear
Where I could see no sign
    Of Thee, but only fear.
Strengthen me, make me to see Thy beauty always
    In every happening here.

IVOR GURNEY

67

Arthur Benjamin, Ivor had an intimate circle with whom he could swap thoughts and dreams. In February 1913 the three young men attended the first London performance of Vaughan Williams's *Sea Symphony*, an experience that left them speechless with joy and one that had a profound influence on Gurney.

Despite the fact that his enthusiastic and passionate nature could never really be disciplined into a formal structure of education, Ivor's songwriting talents were progressing apace, particularly in his five settings of Elizabethan lyrics. He was also taking a serious interest in the English poetry revival led by John Masefield, and his letters to his equally ambitious friend, Will Harvey, were sprinkled with references to the latest literary developments and his own first attempts at composition.

When Ivor Gurney began a spell of creative work he entered into it with body and soul, going without sleep and forgetting to eat — a life-style that undoubtedly contributed to his uncertain mental state. After a period of feverish activity in the spring of 1913 he almost suffered a nervous breakdown and only an escape to Framilode and the healing breezes of Gloucestershire could restore his racked constitution. The summer of 1914 was spent walking the Cotswold lanes, sailing *Dorothy*, his small boat, and visiting old friends. Happy though these returns to Gloucestershire made him, far away from that deceptively carefree figure, who sailed his boat on the untroubled waters of the Severn, world events were conspiring to throw a whirlpool into Ivor Gurney's already unstable life and bring worrying currents to the surface . . .

As soon as war was declared in August 1914, Ivor volunteered for active service, only to be turned down because of his poor eyesight. Nevertheless, when he

volunteered again at the beginning of 1915 he was accepted and drafted into the 2nd/5th Gloucesters. Most of the Army training took place in Chelmsford, an activity that Ivor enjoyed, just as he enthused about the early days in France (his battalion arrived there at the end of May 1916).

As time went by, the inevitable disillusionment set in, and desperately needing a link with the England of home and friendship that he had left behind, Ivor became a compulsive letter-writer. His correspondence sparkled with gentle self-deprecation, humour and bitter irony at the vast waste of so many young lives, but by a strange paradox the war also provided him with a kind of peace and happiness that he had not known before. He delighted in the company of good,

Strange Service

Little did I dream, England, that you bore me
Under the Cotswold hills beside the water meadows,
To do you dreadful service, here, beyond your borders
And your enfolding seas.

I was a dreamer ever, and bound to your dear service,
Meditating deep, I thought on your secret beauty,
As through a child's face one may see the clear spirit
Miraculously shining.

Your hills not only hills, but friends of mine and kindly,
Your tiny knolls and orchards hidden beside the river
Muddy and strongly-flowing, with shy and tiny streamlets
Safe in its bosom.

Now these are memories only, and your skies and rushy sky-pools
Fragile mirrors easily broken by moving airs . . .
In my deep heart for ever goes on your daily being,
And uses consecrate.

Think on me too, O Mother, who wrest my soul to serve you
In strange and fearful ways beyond your encircling waters;
None but you can know my heart, its tears and sacrifice;
None, but you, repay.

IVOR GURNEY

Ivor Gurney (standing left) with other members of the 2nd/5th Gloucester Regiment in 1915.

ordinary men, aware that they were all enduring hardship and danger together. He also experienced the same sense of release from responsibility shared by many soldiers — a feeling that decisions were now being made for him and all he could do was accept it and get on with life.

Astonishing as it may seem, with all the noise and death surrounding him, Ivor did manage to continue composing poetry and songs. His poem "To Certain Comrades" was written in a disused trench-mortar emplacement, as was his setting for John Masefield's "By a Bierside". How he managed to retain enough concentration for such work is remarkable. A constant stream of poems was sent to Marion Scott, anxiously waiting back in England, and at last in July 1917 his first book *Severn and Somme* was accepted for publication by Sidgwick and Jackson.

One of Ivor Gurney's most moving poems, *To his Love*, was written on the battlefield when he received news that his friend Will Harvey was missing, presumed dead. Harvey in fact had been taken prisoner and survived the war, but the power of the poem, with its shocking final image, is painfully real.

He's gone and all our plans
Are useless indeed.
We'll walk no more on Cotswold
Where the sheep feed
Quietly and take no heed.

His body, that was so quick,
Is not as you
Knew it, on Severn river
Under the blue
Driving our small boat through.

You would not know him now . . .
But still he died
Nobly, so cover him over
With violets of pride
Purple from Severn side

Cover him, cover him soon
And with thick-set
Masses of memoried flowers
Hide that red wet
Thing I must somehow forget.

This poem eventually appeared in Ivor's second collection of verse. His favourite, much-missed corner of

The quagmire of Passchendaele, the third Battle of Ypres, in which 400,000 troops died.

England was remembered again and again in Ivor's letters home. He yearned to return there to a normal life:

'O for a garden to dig in, and music and books in a house of one's own, set in a little valley from whose ridges one may see the Malverns and the Welsh Hills, the plain of Severn and the Severn Sea . . . One could grow whole and happy there, the mind would lose its sickness and grow strong . . . I grow happy writing of it.'

Although the war had longer yet to run, Ivor Gurney's part had been played. Gassed and shell-shocked at Passchendaele in 1917 he was sent home to hospital in Edinburgh. He would never be quite the same again. At first his recovery seemed to be progressing well, but the letters to his family and friends suddenly started to take on a disturbing tone. His behaviour rocked precariously between normality and the erratic wanderings that had characterised his life to a lesser extent before the war. He returned to London to continue his scholarship and worked tremendously hard on his songs and verse, often for 24 hours at a stretch.

In 1919 another volume of poetry entitled *War's Embers* was published.

Ivor remained at the Royal College until the summer of 1921, but having failed his Fellowship examination decided to leave and the thin threads that had held his life together were finally dissolved. No regular employment came his way and he drifted from job to job. His loyal friends rallied round to help and the publication of his music was encouraging, but very soon any remaining order to his life collapsed completely. Ivor was committed first to Barnwood House in Gloucester and then to the City of London Mental Hospital near Dartford in Kent.

The agony he suffered at being locked inside all the time is easy to imagine, a distress that the frequent visits from old friends could do little to alleviate. Marion Scott was the most loyal of these and she sometimes took him for drives in her car, including a memorable visit to Dover where the sight of the sea moved the poor man to tears. She it was, too, who took care of Ivor's manuscripts and, together with Herbert Howells and a fellow composer, Gerald Finzi, arranged for their publication.

Ivor Gurney's own great literary hero was Edward Thomas who had himself fought in the First World War and been killed on Easter Monday, 1917. Ivor had set many of Thomas's poems to music and so it was a momentous occasion for him in 1932 when Marion Scott was accompanied on her visit to the Dartford asylum by Thomas's widow, Helen. The encounter also made a deep impression on Helen: the cell-like room with its bare furnishings and barred window; the way that Ivor's face lit up when she spoke about Edward and the English countryside; and the poignant scene just before the ladies left when Ivor played for a group of blank-faced fellow inmates on an old piano.

Helen Thomas visited him again, sometimes noticing a slight improvement in his condition as they chatted about subjects dear to both their hearts. Sadly, moments like that were rare, and black depression was his most frequent companion. His death, at the age of 47, from tuberculosis, came as a merciful release.

Ivor died just as his songs were receiving much wider public recognition and the poems, too, have now taken their rightful place in any serious consideration of modern literature. Although some are rather obscure and unlikely to be widely read, others stand with the very finest of First World War poetry. To those who knew him, the broken figure of Ivor Gurney came to symbolise all the suffering and madness of war, but even as the words were being spoken over his coffin the clouds of yet another conflict were looming, ready to engulf a new generation.

At least, for Ivor Gurney, all suffering and pain were finally over . .

STEPHEN GARNETT

The Songs I Had

The songs I had are withered
Or vanished clean,
Yet there are bright tracks
Where I have been

And there grow flowers
For others' delight.
Think well, O singer,
Soon comes night.

IVOR GURNEY

NOEL HODGSON

(1893–1916)

Thursday, 29th June 1916, might have been an important day in our history, the first day of the Battle of the Somme. But the battle was postponed at the last moment leaving the soldiers with unexpected time on their hands; time to think about the fighting ahead — or to try not to think. The feelings of one young lieutenant appeared in print that day in a poem, "Before Action" (see page 87), which was to become famous. Lieutenant W.N. Hodgson, Bombing Officer of the 9th Battalion of The Devonshire Regiment, was 23 years old. In 11 months of trench warfare he had shown himself to be a good soldier and had earned both a mention in despatches and a Military Cross, but as the months passed illness and grief for friends took their toll. With the battle drawing near he no longer felt like a soldier. He felt young, unprepared and acutely aware of all that he might be about to lose.

Sadly Lieutenant Hodgson's fears were well-founded, for he was killed in action two days later, on 1st July. His battalion was ordered to attack across a complex of German trenches to the south of Mametz village. Their position was unfortunate, particularly on the right where the attacking companies, emerging from the shelter of the trees of Mansel Copse, were completely exposed to enemy machine guns on high ground near the village. In the opening minutes of the attack some of the Devons made rapid progress,

Lieutenant Noel Hodgson. He put into words the feelings of a generation at war.

To a Boy

Oh arrow-straight and slender
With grey eyes unafraid,
You see the roses' splendour
Nor reck that they shall fade.

Youth in its flush and flower
Has a soul of whitest flame,
Eternity in an hour,
All life and death in a game.

May youth for ever weave you
His magic round your ways,
And Time the robber leave you
The boy's heart all your days.

NOEL HODGSON

reaching the third line of German trenches, but this was soon checked as the Germans manned their machine guns, and their bombers moved against the Devons. Hodgson was trying to carry fresh supplies of bombs to his men in the captured trenches when a bullet caught him in the throat, killing him almost instantly. He is buried in Mansel Copse with 162 other men of his regiment who died that day.

Before Action and its tragic aftermath are well known, for the poem is included in most anthologies of First World War poetry, but little has been written about Lieutenant Hodgson himself. He was born in the vicarage at Thornbury in Gloucestershire on 3rd January 1893. His father, Rev. Henry Bernard Hodgson, was vicar of the church of St. Mary the Virgin and his mother was the daughter of an admiral. There were

three older children; eight-year-old Arthur, six-year-old Hal and Stella who was two. The Hodgsons named their fourth child William Noel; "Noel" is the name used in formal records, but to his brothers, sister and friends he was "Bill". In 1897, when he was four, the family moved to Berwick-on-Tweed, where Rev. Henry Hodgson had been appointed vicar of Holy Trinity Church.

This was to be the third clerical appointment in a distinguished career, for Rev. Henry Hodgson's parish work earned him the respect of parishioners and fellow-clergy alike. In February 1914 he became the first Bishop of the new diocese of St. Edmondsbury and Ispwich. He exerted a strong influence over youngest son, Noel, who resembled his father in appearance and character; the two were particularly close. As the boys

The lovely countryside of Cumberland, which had a lasting effect on Noel's outlook on life.

grew up and Arthur and Hal chose their own careers, Rev. Henry Hodgson cherished the hope that Noel would follow him into the Church, as he had followed his own father.

The Hodgsons were a happy family and Noel

looked back fondly on his own childhood. Family holidays were spent in Cumberland where Rev. Henry Hodgson's brother Rev. William Hodgson lived with his wife and five children. Other relatives lived in the area too for the Hodgsons had deep roots in Cumberland, reaching back to the sixteenth century at least. Noel Hodgson knew that he belonged to a long line of Cumbrians and it was important to him. "How the Lakes delighted him", an Oxford friend remembered, "he felt for them as a lover or a child". For him the hills of Cumberland were a reminder of the timelessness of God. In wartime it comforted him to know that these hills had seen other wars, and had seen them pass.

The Hodgson children probably received their early education at home. All four became prolific writers of prose and poetry and Stella later achieved success writing crime novels under the pen name "Faith Wolsley". Noel's brother Hal was a talented artist. When he was 12 years old, Noel won a scholarship to Durham, one of the oldest schools in the country, and began there in September, 1905. The school had close links with the cathedral where boys were required to attend services. For a boy of Hodgson's temperament the school was ideal, and he loved it. The Headmaster remembered him as a rather reserved boy of high academic ability. A good and enthusiastic athlete, he ran and played both rugby and cricket for the school. His liveliness could lead him into mischief; in one of his wartime sketches he recalled climbing from his study window before dawn to go bird's-nesting. They were happy days in Durham reflected by the fact that the school and cathedral often appear in Hodgson's writings as symbols of continuity and peace.

In July 1911 Hodgson left Durham with a scholarship to read Classics at Oxford and entered Christ Church, his father's old college, in October. With the same liveliness of character he had shown at school he threw himself into university life, playing in the hockey and rugby teams and joining the Officers' Training Corps. He found time to join in undergraduate escapades; a friend described how they would climb

Durham Cathedral overlooking the River Wear. Noel attended school in the city.

Christ Church College, Oxford.

the railings early on summer mornings and make off with the college punt — or the punt from some other college! But none of this interfered with his work. As a scholar he was expected to do well, and he disappointed no-one. Friends and teachers were unanimous in praise of his abilities. His tutor's mark book has survived and shows consistently high grades. In 1913 he achieved a First in Honour Moderations.

All of this came to an abrupt end with the outbreak

of war in 1914. As an active OTC member there can have been little doubt that Hodgson would participate, and he joined the 9th Devons on 16th September 1914, but his poems written in the early months of war show little enthusiasm for fighting. He was sure of the rightness of England's position and was anxious to do well himself, but the prevailing mood of his early war poems is one of sadness. He saw that the war would be costly. This touched the Hodgsons very soon; for on 6th November 1914 one of the sons of Noel's uncle was killed in action. He wrote a poem *To a Friend Killed in Action, November 1914*, and he may well have been thinking of his cousin.

Noel Hodgson was in training with his battalion until the summer of 1915, when they were given orders for France. Before their departure he found time to visit Durham and attended Evensong in the cathedral. Anxious as he was, the service touched him deeply and he described his feelings:

Last night dream-hearted in the Abbey's spell
We stood to sing old Simeon's passing hymn,
When sudden splendour of the sunset fell
Full on my eyes, and passed and left all dim —
At once a summons and a deep farewell.

I am content — our life is but a trust
From the great hand of God, and if I keep
The immortal Treasure clean of mortal rust
Against His Claim, 'tis well, and let me sleep
Among the not dishonourable dust.

The battalion sailed for France on 27th July 1915. Within days the 9th Devons were entrenched near Festubert. In England Hodgson had guessed the effects of war; now he saw the effects at first-hand and his poems

△ Noel (second from right) pictured in France with three other officers of the 9th Devons less than a year before his death in 1916.

Before Action

By all the glories of the day and the cool evening's benison,
By that last sunset touch that lay upon the hills when day was done,
By beauty lavishly outpoured and blessings carelessly received,
By all the days that I have lived make me a soldier, Lord.

By all of all man's hopes and fears, and all the wonders poets sing,
The laughter of unclouded years, and every sad and lovely thing;
By the romantic ages stored with high endeavour that was his,
By all his mad catastrophes make me a man, O Lord.

I, that on my familiar hill saw with uncomprehending eyes
A hundred of Thy sunsets spill their fresh and sanguine sacrifice,
Ere the sun swings his noonday sword must say good-bye to all of this;
By all delights that I shall miss, help me to die, O Lord.

NOEL HODGSON

reflect this. He contrasted the peace and beauty of
home with present hardships — the blisters and thirst
of route marching, the devastated countryside, and
soldiers' cemeteries appearing by the roadsides. As
strongly as he had once approved "the pride of those
who live where their fathers died" it now hurt him to
think of men uprooted to die abroad.

In September Hodgson experienced battle for the
first time at Loos. His battalion were in reserve
trenches at first, but moved forward soon after fighting began, at 6.30 on the morning of the 25th. Finding
communication trenches blocked they moved forward in the open which exposed them to enemy fire.
The situation became confused with parties of men
holding different positions in captured trenches.

Barbed wire entangles the end of a trench on the Western Front.

Hodgson was with one of these groups: four inexperienced young officers and about 100 men who managed to hold their ground under enemy fire and counter-attacks. They were cut off from reinforcement and rations until the evening of the 26th. Hodgson wrote a vivid prose account of these events, and for his part in the battle he was awarded the MC.

Sensitive, scholarly and rather reserved, Noel Hodgson may not have seemed ideal material for the army, yet his record shows that he acquitted himself well, and he was well thought of. In his poems he expressed emotions he did not show, and very few people were aware that he wrote. For publication he always used the name "Edward Melbourne". In public he was cheerful and dependable and friends in the battalion called him "Smiler". In the 1920s survivors of the 9th Devons still remembered this one lieutenant among so many. The Regimental History, which pays few personal tributes, says he was "a fine officer, a most inspiring personality with a great hold on his men".

Hodgson expressed his emotions, ideals and faith in poetry. To describe the experience of war he turned to prose, writing short sketches of trench warfare for such publications as *The Spectator, The Saturday Review* and *The Yorkshire Post.* From February 1916 onwards he wrote almost weekly, giving a clear and honest account of life in and around the trenches. He had an eye for detail and a gift for descriptive writing, and his prose included irony and humour, elements almost absent from his poems. The sketches describe Loos and the period following, when the battalion was rebuilding both itself and the trenches in the Fricourt/ Mametz area in preparation for the Somme.

William Noel Hodgson died at 23 years old. No-one can tell what he would have achieved had he lived. He was gifted academically and in person. People liked and remembered him and those who knew his work at Durham and Oxford were sure he was destined for a distinguished career, perhaps in the Church as his father wished, or some other sphere. His writings deserve to be remembered as evidence of their times and for their own merits. They leave an impression of one who was, in the words of a friend, "simple, fearless and wonderfully alive".

C.M. ZEEPVAT.

The author of this haunting poem, T.P. Cameron Wilson, was a schoolmaster before the outbreak of the First World War. He became a captain in the Sherwood Foresters and was killed in France in 1918.

Magpies in Picardy

The magpies in Picardy
Are more than I can tell.
They flicker down the dusty roads
And cast a magic spell
On the men who march through Picardy,
Through Picardy to hell.

The blackbird flies with panic,
The swallow goes with light,
The finches move like ladies,
The owl floats by at night;
But the great and flashing magpie
He flies as artists might.

A magpie in Picardy
Told me secret things —
Of the music in white feathers,
And the sunlight that sings
And dances in deep shadows —
He told me with his wings.

The hawk is cruel and rigid,
He watches from a height;
The rook is slow and sombre,
The robin loves to fight;
But the great and flashing magpie
He flies as lovers might.

He told me that in Picardy,
An age ago or more,
While all his fathers still were eggs,
These dusty highways bore
Brown, singing soldiers marching out
Through Picardy to war.

He said that still through chaos
Works on the ancient plan,
And two things have altered not
Since first the world began —
The beauty of the wild green earth
And the bravery of man.

For the sparrow flies unthinking
And quarrels in his flight;
The heron trails his legs behind,
The lark goes out of sight;
But the great and flashing magpie
He flies as poets might.

Ernest Raymond, whose writing career spanned both world wars.

ERNEST RAYMOND

(1888-1974)

E rnest Raymond, the First World War padre
and poet who became a best-selling novelist,
twice shocked the establishment — first by giving up his priesthood, and secondly by becoming an
agnostic. But the man who thrilled millions of readers
with a series of best-sellers had other surprises in store
before his life drew to a close at the age of 85.

Born a century ago — on New Year's Eve, 1888 —
of "irregular parentage" he describes the unusual circumstances of his childhood in the first volume of his
autobiography *The Story of My Days*. He was
brought up in the West London suburb of Brook
Green, by an irascible aunt. Other members of the
household included a little girl called "Dots", a year
older than himself, and Major General Frederick
Blake, late of the Royal Marine Light Infantry, whom
the children called "Dum". He was as kind to them as
Aunt Emily was hard and Ernest loved and admired
him throughout his life, though it was not until he was
about 15 that he discovered that Dum was really his
father, and Aunt Emily's sister Ida was his mother.
Having been born out of wedlock (in Switzerland) he
was given the name Raymond to shield his mother
from shame.

In spite of her fiery temper, Aunt Emily was a keen
churchgoer and close friend of the vicar of the nearby

Anglican church. Through frequent attendance there Ernest learned to love the sonorous phrases of the liturgical services. He had a great feeling for words and delighted in Dum's fondness for reading aloud. When he was nine he conceived a desire to write and began to keep a diary but, childlike, he did not keep it up for long.

Though shy and dreamy, Ernest was clever and did well at his first school, Colet Court, a preparatory for St. Paul's. Perhaps as a result of his uncertain home background he had a fierce desire to be liked while at first finding it difficult to make friends. In the entrance examination for St. Paul's, Ernest did well enough to be placed in the scholarship class where he received a concentrated classical education at the hands of an eccentric but brilliant master, Elam, who in addition to making him expert in writing Latin poetry and Greek prose, taught him to think for himself. Years later, Ernest fictionalised his schooldays at St. Paul's in his novel *Mr. Olim* and paid tribute to his former master as well as to the High Man himself, the grey-bearded, silk-gowned, mighty-voiced and awesome F.W. Walker.

Holidays were taken in Boulogne, where his aunt's family had connections, and at Freshwater, Isle of Wight, where Dum owned a holiday house. One idyllic holiday, when Ernest was 11, was spent with his father at the Grand Hotel, Brighton. Dum bought him an expensive new suit for the occasion and they travelled First Class. There was always a special relationship between the two of them. Dum called Ernest "Mr. Koko" when he was little and even after he discovered his father's deception Raymond regarded him as his hero and believed him to be fundamentally a good man. Sadly, the following year Dum left them all and

Ernest's father, Frederick Blake or "Dum", whom Ernest adored.

the children saw him only occasionally. When four years later the General died, Ernest was heart-broken.

There was no love lost between Ernest and his Aunt Emily and although in the terms of General Blake's will provision was made for Ernest's education she decided to economise by taking him away from St. Paul's, where he was expected to get a scholarship to Oxbridge, and sent him to a cheap boarding school. There he found no intellectual stimulus and made little progress. Eventually after three wasted terms he was allowed to leave and take a job in the office of the Army & Navy Stores at ten shillings a week. By this time Ernest had finally decided he wished to be a writer. Feeling that clerical work would get him nowhere he obtained a post at a prep school coaching boys in Classics for entrance to Winchester. He proved a successful teacher but in his second school, at Bath, he became strongly attracted to Anglo-Catholicism and decided to take Holy Orders. In 1912 he went to Chichester Theological College and did brilliantly. In retrospect, Ernest realised he entered the Church from mixed and self-regarding motives. He wanted to prove himself academically, as he had been deprived of a university education, and also subconsciously he felt that as a priest he might have more leisure for writing, for by now he was determined to win fame as a novelist.

On Trinity Sunday 1914, three weeks before Archduke Franz Ferdinand of Austria was assassinated at Sarajevo, Ernest was made deacon and became a priest a year later at the age of 26. Although holding a curacy at Southend, he immediately volunteered for service overseas as an Army chaplain.

Characteristically of the young of his generation he waited impatiently for a posting, while on a short holiday in Falmouth, hoping that the war would not be

Ernest and Aunt Emily, who was very strict.

A 60-pounder gun in action during the Dardanelles campaign.

over too soon and he be deprived of what he believed would be the greatest experience of his life. As a chaplain he would be non-combatant, but at that time he did not know that the life expectancy of a junior officer in France or Gallipoli was about 14 days!

On reading in *The Times* Sir Ian Hamilton's despatch from Gallipoli, reporting the gallant assault on the West Beach of the peninsula by the 1st Battalion of the Lancashire Fusiliers, Ernest was reminded of Homer's account of the Siege of Troy. He was thrilled with the classical setting of the Gallipoli Campaign and hoped he would be posted to the Dardanelles. His wish was fulfilled, and after being kitted out with a complete officer's uniform of which he was inordinately proud, he found himself in the troopship *Scotian* heading for Lemnos, Helles and finally West Beach and the famous hill Achi Baba where he was to join the 42nd Division of the East Lancashire Territorials.

As a chaplain, Ernest showed great love and compassion for the men in his care and had an easy relationship with them, but he was disappointed that his position as padre was a conventional one — preaching at Parade Services and writing letters for the wounded or dying. The Sacraments of Holy Communion and Penance, which at this time he considered of supreme importance, were not much in demand. One of his more harrowing rôles was that of burial officer. On Lemnos he officiated at the grave of Charles Lister, Lord Ribblesdale's son and a friend of Rupert Brooke. Lister had organised Rupert's burial with full military honours on the island of Skyros, but for him no guns were fired or the Last Post sounded. His body was borne on a mule waggon and his resting place a lonely acre on a stony barren plain. Like Rupert Brooke, God had "matched him for this hour" and he too had found "the worst friend and enemy is but death".

> *O Death, thou poor and disappointed thing —*
> *Strike if thou wilt and soon; strike breast and brow*
> *For I have lived and thou canst rob me now*
> *Only of some long life that ne'er has been*
> *The life that I have lived so full, so keen,*
> *Is mine! I hold firm beneath thy blow*
> *And, dying, take it with me where I go.*
>
> (*Preface to* Tell England)

Ernest Raymond's ambition to write novels was still very much alive. He had already written chapters of a story based on his own schooldays and experiences as a schoolmaster, but the war had intervened. Now he decided to extend the book showing how his own generation passed within a year or two from a carefree life at school into the holocaust of war. In his book the scene of the conflict would be the Gallipoli

Peninsula, a classical background of islands in a wine-dark sea. The title of his book *Tell England* he derived from the immortal words of the epitaph on the Spartans who fell at Thermopylae:

Go, tell the Spartans, thou who passest by,
That here obedient to their laws we lie.

When the abortive campaign against the Turks on Gallipoli failed, the British Force was successfully evacuated. Ernest was one of the lucky ones, but 1,000 dead were left behind. The Cricket Match was over for them and the last man out, but the war was by no means over for Ernest Raymond, though at first the conflict for him was less intense. In 1917 to his great satisfaction his division was sent to France where they took part in the Third Ypres Campaign at Passchendaele, marching through the Menin Gate to "Hell Fire Corner" and into the liquid mud, bombardments, gas and bombs. After about three weeks in the salient he was requested to volunteer for service in Mesopotamia where a big offensive was imminent. He had now been transferred to the 9th Worcesters. At first life was easy and he gave the time to writing his Gallipoli book in Army Field Service notebooks, but soon the order came to advance 100 miles to Kirkuk, held by the Turks. When they were driven out, Ernest and other officers were deputed to tend the sick and wounded whom the Turks had left behind. The filth and stench of that hospital was indescribable.

The last leg of his war-time service took him to Persia. After Kirkuk, his division was sent to join Major General Dunsterville of the Hush-hush Brigade to protect the Armenian population of Baku. When Baku fell to the Turks and they were ordered to evacuate, Ernest forgot his precious manuscript of *Tell England*.

Consecration

Watch. Means it nothing to our handicraft
That God has chosen for his earthly throne
No pure and lovely output of his own;
That fire and wind and water do not waft
Down to our waiting eyes his kingly shape,
But rather he has deigned to set his feet
In bread which men have fashioned from the wheat
And wine, their human product of the grape?

So prospers he our handicraft. And lo,
Whether we rule the world or plough the soil,
Build symphonies or break the crusted sod,
Or strive to frame our thoughts in song, we know
Creation labours in the daily toil,
That works may prosper, being filled with God.

ERNEST RAYMOND

Luckily, the order was given to return to their camp and he was able to retrieve it.

Five months after the signing of the Armistice, he was demobbed and in 1919 he returned to civilian life as curate at Brighton parish church. During that year he prepared *Tell England* for publication. In the next six months he tried a dozen publishers without success. When, in 1922, it was finally published by Cassells many critics condemned it as sentimental and loosely written (on re-reading it 40 years later Ernest

Raymond rather agreed with them!). He called himself "a Victorian sentimentalist", yet in spite of an inauspicious launching *Tell England* became an immediate best-seller — 300,000 copies were sold.

The success of the book strengthened his desire to make writing novels his profession. His experience as a chaplain may have weakened his faith in the importance of specifically Anglo-Catholic teaching. He had accepted it naïvely and uncritically, having fallen in

love with the beauty of its ceremonial and worship, but after the trauma of war he began to question fundamental doctrines of the Creed and he felt hypocritical when preaching and teaching candidates for Confirmation. He was suffering from "spiritual insolvency", so took the almost unheard of step of applying for permission to leave the priesthood and a Deed of Relinquishment was reluctantly granted by the Bishop of Chichester in 1928. For the next 40 years Ernest Raymond called himself an agnostic but firmly refuted the idea that he was an atheist.

During the following decade he devoted himself to establishing his reputation as a novelist. In the period up to the Second World War he produced no less than 15 novels and in spite of his rejection of orthodox Anglicanism nearly all his books have an underlying Christian philosophy. They show also his great love and sympathy for his fellows and solidarity with their weaknesses. This is especially evident in the book which won him a prestigious literary award, the Book Guild Gold Medal, and has proved of lasting popularity though published as long ago as 1935. If any book could have influenced the British public to renounce the death penalty surely it is *We The Accused.* It is also an implied criticism of the whole legal system and the public's appetite for scandal.

Shortly after the publication of *Tell England* Ernest had married Zoë Doucett. The marriage was not entirely successful but they remained together until their two children, Patrick and Lella, were old enough to make their own way in life. In 1940 the marriage was dissolved and Ernest married his second wife, Diana Young, this time for life. They first met at a meeting of the young P.E.N. Club of which he had been President since 1933. In this rôle Ernest led a delegation to Czechoslovakia just before the Second World War broke out. In Prague he talked with Benes and Karel Capek and was deeply disturbed by their country's fate. He was appalled at Chamberlain's so-called "peace with honour". When at length the decision was made to resist Hitler's unprovoked attack on Poland, Ernest was relieved and almost glad. It was a weight off the country's conscience and he experienced a certain pleasure and excitement. Once more, as in the days of *Tell England*, he could be proud of the integrity that lay hidden in the beauty of his native land — its fields and lanes and villages. He recorded his feelings in his *Secret of England* which he wrote in the autumn of 1939.

As it turned out, Ernest's own experience in the Second World War was less dramatic than he had hoped. When war was declared he offered his services to the Ministry of Information, as at the age of 51 he was too

(Continued on page 106)

The peak of Roseberry Topping beckons a passing walker in the Cleveland Hills of Yorkshire.

The Secret of England
by Ernest Raymond

I sing no song of England,
My wits are slow and dry;
I only rise to help her
And, rising, wonder why.
Why beats my heart for England?
You wiser men may know.
I know this only, brothers:
She calls me and I go!

The secret that is England
Her long green pastures kept;
Her quiet hamlets store it;
Her hills that seem asleep
Enfold it in the valleys
With ploughland, park, and wood.
Her milk-white mists enshroud it,
And know that it is good.

These sing the song of England,
Whose words I cannot hear;
I only know they build for me
A meaning that is dear.
They sing perhaps her sage old soul
That slowly toils to find
The way to freedom, faithfulness,
And laughter that is kind.

Oh, she has sins a-plenty,
And her broad green breast is scarred . . .
But the hills that girdle England
Keep a truth that I shall guard.

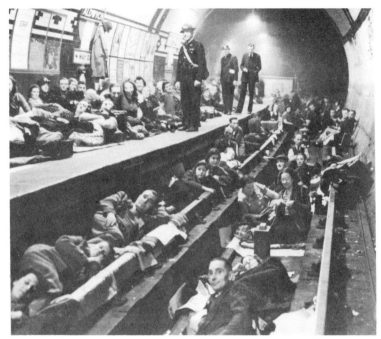

Underground stations became home to thousands of Londoners during the Blitz.

(Continued from page 103)

old for military service, but was rejected. So as soon as it was inaugurated he volunteered for the Home Guard in Hampstead, where he was then living. He describes his experiences in the Force in his essay *An Old Platoon* — the trauma of the Blitz and the heart-break of Londoners nightly trekking to the Underground stations for shelter. When the end of the war in Europe was followed by the horror of Hiroshima, Ernest's enthusiasm for England's heroism in leaping to the defence of freedom gave place to revulsion and he was moved to write what he considered the Christian approach to conflict should be: vengeance was wrong and mercy and pity were the only possible expression of applied Christianity. From henceforth this had to be the theme of his novels, but it was a private rather than a national pacifism which he advocated, yet without preaching. He believed that if he was true to his intuitive perception of Christian pacifism there was bound to be some "fall-out" in his novels.

For those who fought in Flanders, on the Somme, and many other arenas in the Great War, the experience was the most tremendous and unforgettable of their lives. Ernest Raymond felt a great solidarity with old soldiers who continued to return to the scene of those conflicts, as he himself had served alongside them in both Gallipoli and France. He planned to write a novel about them. Having been present at Passchendaele he decided to revisit this one-time theatre of war and at the same time perhaps discover the grave of his wife's father, killed near Hill 60 in 1917. For the second time, therefore, though in very different circumstances, he found himself wandering along the Menin Road between rows of tall poplars, once the salient, now no longer knee-deep in mud but a green landscape with cows peacefully grazing. He enquired at the Ypres office of the Commonwealth War Graves Commission and found the grave of William Thomas Young, Royal Garrison Artillery, killed in action 12.7.17, aged 36. It was at Brandhoek Military Cemetery among the serried ranks of white grave stones, but there were 50,000 British dead whose bodies were never found. These are remembered every evening at 9pm at the Menin Gate Memorial where their names are inscribed. Two young firemen from Ypres on silver bugles sound the Last Post.

> *Tell England ye who pass this Monument*
> *We died for her and here we rest content.*

During the last decade of his life he continued to

The Menin Gate Memorial, where soldiers whose bodies were never found are commemorated each evening.

write novels. His last book was written in 1973, the year before he died, but he found time for many peaceful activities. He went rock-climbing in Cumberland and he loved watching cricket. One of the most significant events of his latter years was a visit to the Holy Land. Over a long period of time he had been recovering his faith in the teaching of the Church and the Divinity of Christ and he describes this in his novel *The Bethany Road.*

Before he died in 1974 Ernest Raymond ended his 40 years' sojourn in the wilderness of agnosticism. In the

Ernest in his later days, working in his study.

end it was the conviction that only love can conquer evil which brought him back to the Christian faith. Perhaps because his childhood was largely devoid of affection, he was obsessed throughout his life with man's need for love and with compassion for those who were deprived of it. This is evident in the way he lived and in his novels. He believed the task of a novelist to be not primarily that of an entertainer but by presenting the comedy, tragedy and heroism of human life to arouse his readers' pity and understanding. Man's capacity to love and be loved could have its source only in God, because we are made in His image. In the Holy Land, Ernest Raymond came face-to-face with the source of reciprocal love — God giving his only-begotten Son, because He so loved the world.

ELIZABETH SAINTSBURY

WILFRED OWEN

(1893-1918)

On an autumn morning over 70 years ago — at 11 o'clock on the 11th of November 1918 — England suddenly went into a frenzy. As Big Ben struck the hour, sending its thunderous echoes booming across London, it was joined by scores of sirens, factory hooters and steam-train whistles in a deafening cacophony of noise. Shrugging off their usual Monday morning gloom, people poured out of their places of work until the streets were blocked with cheering and singing crowds.

The scene was the same wherever you went in England, with church bells in every town and village adding their own voices to the symphony of celebration that swept across the country like a line of blazing beacons. Germany had been defeated, the Armistice had been signed that very morning, and at long last the First World War — the most costly conflict in terms of human life that history has ever seen — was finally over.

Sadly, in the midst of all this jubilation there were many people — those who had lost much-loved fathers, husbands, brothers and sons — who felt unable to join in the general merriment. All they had

Wilfred Owen, probably the most gifted soldier-poet of all.

Plas Wilmot at Oswestry, the house where Wilfred was born in the upstairs room on the right.

to keep their memories company were sepia photo-graphs of proud young soldiers and bundles of their precious letters sent home from the Front.

A father and mother most cruelly touched in this way were Tom and Susan Owen of 71 Monkmoor Road, Shrewsbury. Even as the pealing bells of the town's many churches were joyfully proclaiming the good news, a single solemn chime on the Owens' front door-bell signalled the arrival of a telegram. It told them that their eldest son Wilfred, a 25-year-old lieutenant in the Manchester Regiment, had been kil-led just one week before the Armistice while trying to get his men across the Sambre Canal.

It was a terrible blow, particularly as he had so nearly made it through the war. Although they had

Wilfred's family at Plas Wilmot in 1895. Wilfred is on his mother's knee, next to Grandfather Shaw. The others in the group are Aunt Emma Gunston and her family.

three other children, Susan had always been especially devoted to Wilfred and in his letters home he had told her all of his innermost thoughts and hopes. She knew of his passion for poetry, but neither Susan nor Tom could have guessed that within a few years he would be regarded, not only as the finest poet of the First World War, but as the author of some of the most evocative verse in the English language.

Wilfred Edward Salter Owen was born on 18th March, 1893, at "Plas Wilmot", the home that Tom and Susan shared with Susan's father in Owestry, Shropshire. It was a happy childhood in every respect, even though financial difficulties following the death of the old man in 1897 forced the family to sell their grand house with most of its possessions and look for somewhere more modest. Tom was an administrator with the Joint Railway Company and the next few years saw the family moving back and forth between

A corner of old Shrewsbury.

Birkenhead and Shrewsbury. At the end of 1906 Tom was appointed Assistant Superintendent with the GW and LNER, Western Region, and the family was at last able to settle in Shropshire again, first at 1 Cleveland Place, Shrewsbury, and then in Monkmoor Road. By this time the other children had been born (Mary,

Harold and Colin) and as he was the eldest Wilfred was often put in charge of them. The teachers at both of Wilfred's schools, the Birkenhead Institute and Shrewsbury Technical School, were extremely impressed with Wilfred — a rather serious, delicately built little boy, with a shock of brown hair and a very bright mind.

Harold had to share a bed with his older brother and in later life described how Wilfred, while still a schoolboy, would work late into the night by the light of a guttering candle:

> 'I did not mind so much when he was writing but when he was reading I found myself waiting, with held breath, for the turning of each page. From time to time I could lie still no longer; Wilfred, without turning or stopping what he was doing, would exclaim with savage irritation: "Oh, do go to sleep, you stupid boy. I cannot work unless you do." On other nights he would pace the eight feet or so of the minute room, declaiming aloud or memorizing in a mumble. Hours later would come the painful business as he inserted his cold and shaking body into the bed; his chattering teeth would keep me awake after he himself had fallen into exhausted sleep.'

They were a close family, even if Mary and the scholarly Wilfred tended to gravitate more towards the protective wing of their mother, while the boisterous Harold and Colin were happier in the company of their father. Before marrying Susan, Tom Owen had worked in India and he never tired of telling his children about the adventurous sea voyages he had made — romanticising them a little for the extra delight of his children. He encouraged them in outdoor pursuits, teaching them to swim and supervising their own attempts at seafaring — even if it was only sailing model yachts on the local pond! There were also memorable family holidays in Cornwall and Yorkshire. Keen to get to know his book-loving son better, on a couple of occasions Tom took Wilfred across the Channel to Brittany. Back home in Shropshire, the family discovered the delightful village of Uffington and it was not unusual for Tom, accompanied by one or more of the children, to tramp there on warm summer evenings, crossing the River Severn by ferry and attending evensong in the little village church.

By the time he was 17, although he still didn't know what he wanted to do with his life, he was passionately interested in poetry and had started composing his own verse. His great hero was John Keats, and on a visit to Teignmouth in Devon he sought out the house in Northumberland Place where the Romantic poet had once lived. The present residents of the house were quite disturbed to see a 17-year-old youth staring so intently at them through the window! The visit resulted in a sonnet entitled *At Teignmouth, on a Pilgrimage to Keats's House.*

During the summer of 1911, Wilfred worked as pupil-teacher at the Wyle Cop School in Shrewsbury while studying to take the University of London matriculation examination. This he did on 9th September, but was disappointed a month later to learn that, although he had passed, it was not with the hoped-for honours. So instead of following a university career he reluctantly accepted the unpaid post of lay assistant and pupil to the Reverend Herbert Wigan, vicar of Dunsden, Berkshire. Wilfred worked hard while there but he was not happy and in the summer of 1913 he went to France as a teacher of English at the Berlitz School in Bordeaux. This was followed by a period as tutor to two boys in a Catholic family. Despite loving

Teignmouth, Devon, where Wilfred found inspiration.

life in France, when war broke out he witnessed the suffering of wounded soldiers at first-hand in a Bordeaux hospital, which sent him into something of an emotional whirlpool. After a great deal of soul-searching, and the realisation that for his future peace of mind he could not stay out of the conflict, he returned to England and joined the Artists' Rifles. Whilst in London he visited the Poetry Bookshop in Devonshire

The officers of the 5th (reserve) Manchester Regiment at Witley Camp, July 1916. Wilfred is in the front row, second from right.

Futility

Move him into the sun —
Gently its touch awoke him once,
At home, whispering of fields unsown.
Always it woke him, even in France,
Until this morning and this snow.
If anything might rouse him now
The kind old sun will know.

Think how it wakes the seeds, —
Woke, once, the clays of a cold star.
Are limbs, so dear-achieved, are sides,
Full-nerved — still warm — too hard to stir?
Was it for this the clay grew tall?
— O what made fatuous sunbeams toil
To break earth's sleep at all?

WILFRED OWEN

Street, a popular meeting-place for writers and artists, and made friends with Harold Monro, publisher of the influential *Poetry Review*.

Joining up brought tremendous relief to Wilfred and he enjoyed the Army, training at Hare Hall Camp in Essex. It was during his time there, in November 1915, that Edward Thomas arrived at the camp as a private in the Artists' Rifles. Thomas, who was to fall at Arras on Easter Monday, 1917, wrote several of the poems for which he is remembered whilst at Hare Hall, but it seems that the two men never actually met. On 4th June, 1916, Wilfred was commissioned into the Manchester Regiment as 2nd Lieutenant and reported to his battalion at Milford Camp near Whitley, Surrey. His brother, Harold, now in the Merchant

Navy, frequently visited Wilfred and was quick to notice the changes that Army life had effected on the personality of his previously grave and rather intolerant brother. He was now much more patient and at ease with himself.

On 30th December, 1916, Wilfred sailed for France, first going to Base Camp at Étaples, then joining the 2nd Manchesters on the Somme near Beaumont Hamel. It was a baptism of fire. On 12th January 1917, he led his platoon to the Front, having been ordered to hold a dugout in the middle of No Man's Land. They remained at the Front throughout January, in danger, not only from the exploding shells and rattling machine-gun fire, but also from the snow, bitterly cold winds and threat of disease that constantly stalked the trenches.

Soon after a bout of concussion, caused by a fall, Wilfred was found to be suffering from shell-shock. He was sent back to Britain to Craiglockhart War Hospital near Edinburgh, and there it was that one of the most significant events of his life took place — a meeting with another war poet, and one of his great literary heroes, Siegfried Sassoon, whose book *The Old Huntsman* Owen particularly admired. Sassoon, who was also a patient, described his first meeting with Owen, when the latter came nervously into his room:

'Short, dark-haired, and shyly hesitant, he stood for a moment before coming across to the window, where I was sitting on my bed cleaning my golf clubs. A favourable first impression was made by the fact that he had under his arm several copies of *The Old Huntsman*. He had come, he said, hoping that I would be so gracious as to inscribe them for himself and some of his friends . . . He had a charming, honest smile,

Anthem for Doomed Youth

What passing-bells for these who die as cattle?
Only the monstrous anger of the guns.
Only the stuttering rifles' rapid rattle
Can patter out their hasty orisons.
No mockeries now for them; no prayers nor bells;
Nor any voice of mourning save the choirs, —
The shrill, demented choirs of wailing shells;
And bugles calling for them from sad shires.

What candles may be held to speed them all?
Not in the hands of boys but in their eyes
Shall shine the holy glimmers of goodbyes.
The pallor of girls' brows shall be their pall;
Their flowers the tenderness of patient minds,
And each slow dusk a drawing-down of blinds.

WILFRED OWEN

and his manners — he stood at my elbow rather as though conferring with a superior officer — were modest and ingratiating.'

The two became firm friends, and under Sassoon's

Wilfred with a young friend in July 1917.

influence and advice, Wilfred's experiments with poetry fused with his wish to tell people in England about the real horrors of the war, to produce his greatest poems. He set out his aims in a statement that was intended to form the introduction to a planned book of his verse. It became one of the most famous literary declarations of the 20th century:

> This book is not about heroes. English poetry is not yet fit to speak of them. Nor is it about deeds, or lands, nor anything about glory, honour, might, majesty,

dominion, or power, except War. Above all I am not concerned with poetry. My subject is War, and the pity of War. The poetry is in the pity. Yet these elegies are to this generation in no sense consolatory. They may be to the next. All a poet can do today is warn. That is why the true poets must be truthful . . .

Wilfred's wish to stir compassion and truthfully depict the conditions in France found powerful expression in such poems as *Anthem for Doomed Youth, Strange Meeting* and *The Send Off*. There was also that masterpiece of controlled anger *Dulce et Decorum Est* which nailed many of the lies that were being told to English children about the war. It also contained the nightmarish scene that Wilfred must have witnessed many times:

> *Gas! Gas! Quick, boys! — An ecstasy of fumbling,*
> *Fitting the clumsy helmets just in time;*
> *But someone still was yelling out and stumbling*
> *And flound'ring like a man in fire or lime . . .*
> *Dim, through the misty panes and thick green light,*
> *As under a green sea, I saw him drowning.*

The world was now opening up for Wilfred and through Sassoon he made friends with many of the literary figures of the day, including Robert Graves, Arnold Bennett and H.G. Wells. Before these friendships could be cemented, however, he was back at the Front, sad in some ways, but glad to be alongside his men once more. During an attack on the night of 1st/2nd October 1918, when Wilfred's company commander was wounded and he was forced to take charge, Wilfred fought so bravely that he was awarded the Military Cross.

He was fighting just as bravely at the head of his men a month later when he was hit by a German bullet and killed. It was 4th November, 1918. Seven days later the Armistice was declared . . . and that dreaded telegram arrived at the Owen home in Shrewsbury. In the following year several of Wilfred Owen's poems were included in a collection of verse entitled *Wheels*, and then in 1920 came *Poems of Wilfred Owen* with an introduction by Siegfried Sassoon.

On Armistice Day, Harold Owen was on board a ship off the coast of Africa. Going down to his cabin he was amazed to "see" Wilfred, dressed in army uniform, sitting on one of the chairs. He asked him how he had got there, but Wilfred made no reply and sat there for several minutes, smiling gently at his dumbfounded brother. Harold turned away for a moment . . . and when he looked again Wilfred had vanished. "I went into a deep oblivious sleep", wrote Harold later. "When I woke up I knew with absolute certainty that Wilfred was dead."

STEPHEN GARNETT

Dulce Et Decorum Est

Bent double, like old beggars under sacks,
Knock-kneed, coughing like hags, we cursed through sludge,
Till on the haunting flares we turned our backs
And towards our distant rest began to trudge.
Men marched asleep. Many had lost their boots
But limped on, blood-shod. All went lame; all blind;
Drunk with fatigue; deaf even to the hoots
Of tired, outstripped Five-Nines that dropped behind.

Gas! Gas! Quick, boys! — An ecstacy of fumbling,
Fitting the clumsy helmets just in time;
But someone still was yelling out and stumbling,
And flound'ring like a man in fire or lime . . .
Dim, through the misty panes and thick green light,
As under a green sea, I saw him drowning.
In all my dreams, before my helpless sight,
He plunges at me, guttering, choking, drowning.

If in some smothering dreams you too could pace
Behind the wagon that we flung him in,
And watch the white eyes writhing in his face,
His hanging face, like a devil's sick of sin;
If you could hear, at every jolt, the blood
Come gargling from the froth-corrupted lungs,
Obscene as cancer, bitter as the cud
Of vile, incurable sores on innocent tongues, —
My friend, you would not tell with such high zest
To children ardent for some desperate glory,
The old Lie: *Dulce et decorum est
Pro patria mori.*

WILFRED OWEN

A drink and a splash for the horses after a day's work on the farm.

Going Home Together

Over the seas in India the sun was dropping low,
With tramp and creak and jingle I heard the gun teams go,
And something seemed to 'mind me a-dreaming as I lay
Of my own old Hampshire village at the quiet end of day.

Brown thatch with gardens blooming, with lily and white rose,
And the cool, brimming river so pleasant where it flows.
Wide fields of oats and barley and elder flowers like foam,
And the sky gold with sunset, and the horses going home.

Home lads home, all among the corn and clover,
Home lads home, when the working day is over,
Oh, there's rest for horse and man when the longest day is done
And they go home together at the setting of the sun.

Old 'Captain', 'Boxer' and 'Traveller', I see them all so plain,
With tasselled ear-caps nodding along the leafy lane,
There's a bird somewhere calling and the swallows flying low,
And the lads sitting sideways and singing as they go.

Well gone is many a lad now, and many a horse gone too,
Of all the lads and horses in those old fields I knew,
Like Dick that fell at Givenchy, and 'Prince' beside the guns,
On that red road of glory a mile or two from Mons . . .

Dead lads and shadowy horses, I see them just the same,
I see them and I know them and name them each by name,
Going down to quiet waters when all the west's aglow,
And the lads sitting sideways and singing as they go.

Home lads home, with the sunset on their faces,
Home lads home, in the quiet happy places,
Oh, there's rest for horse and man when the longest day is done . . .
And they go home together at the setting of the sun

AUTHOR UNKNOWN

VIVIAN ROSEWARNE

(1916-1940)

The airman whose letter
to his mother touched the
hearts of millions

The outlook was bleak. It was 1940, England
was at war, and even hope itself seemed about
to fail as hundreds of soldiers were evacuated
from Dunkirk. Then, on 18th June, *The Times*
printed a letter that brought inspiration to thousands
of its readers, filling their hearts with hope and the
renewed conviction that they were fighting for freedom and a better world. It would all be worth it in the
end.

The letter had been written by a young RAF Wel-
lington bomber pilot, Vivian Rosewarne, who had
directed that it be sent to his mother in the event of his
death. He had been reported missing on 31st May,
1940, and the letter had been found in his belongings
by the station commander of RAF Marham, Norfolk,
Group Captain C. Hilton Keith. The letter had

touched him so deeply that he had asked Mrs. Rosewarne's permission to have it published anonymously. After it appeared in *The Times*, so many people wrote asking for a copy that Duttons printed it in book form and it had run into its sixth printing by November of that year.

Vivian Rosewarne was born on 5th April, 1916, in East Dulwich, London. He studied at the London Choir School and Brentwood School in Essex, and became fascinated with flying. In 1936, while working as a junior clerk with a Stock Exchange firm, he managed to obtain a short service commission in the RAF and from then on he lived for flying.

His death came as a great shock to all who knew him, but his letter to his mother comforted millions more — so many, in fact, that Mrs. Rosewarne had to issue a card to correspondents as they were too numerous to answer personally. But she was proud to know that her son's words had reached people all over the world — in all walks of life — including the Royal Family, from whom she received the following letter:

> The King wishes... to let you know how deeply moved he was after reading the recent anonymous letter in *The Times* which His Majesty understands was written to you by your son while on active service.
>
> The sentiments which he expressed with such simplicity will, the King is sure, bring inspiration to the young as well as comfort to their parents in these days of stress.

Vivian's hope of contributing something worthwhile to the cause of freedom had been fulfilled in a greater way than he had ever imagined.

PETER BARRYMORE

The letter written by Vivian Rosewarne to his mother is reproduced over the page. ▷

AN AIRMAN TO HIS MOTHER

(First published in *The Times*, June 18th, 1940)

Dearest Mother,

Though I feel no premonition at all, events are moving rapidly and I have instructed that this letter be forwarded to you should I fail to return from one of the raids which we shall shortly be called upon to undertake. You must hope on for a month, but at the end of that time you must accept the fact that I have handed my task over to the extremely capable hands of my comrades of the Royal Air Force, as so many splendid fellows have already done.

First, it will comfort you to know that my role in this war has been of the greatest importance. Our patrols far out over the North Sea have helped to keep the trade routes clear for our convoys and supply ships, and on one occasion our information was instrumental in saving the lives of the men in a crippled lighthouse relief ship. Though it will be difficult for you, you will disappoint me if you do not at least try to accept the facts dispassionately, for I shall have done my duty to the utmost of my ability. No man can do more, and no one calling himself a man could do less.

I have always admired your amazing courage in the face of continual setbacks; in the way you have given me as good an education and background as anyone in the country; and always kept up appearances without ever losing faith in the future. My death would not mean that your struggle has been in vain. Far from it. It means that your sacrifice is as great as mine. Those who serve England must expect nothing from her; we debase ourselves if we regard our country as merely a place in which to eat and sleep.

History resounds with illustrious names who have given all, yet their sacrifice has resulted in the British Empire, where there is a measure of peace, justice and freedom for all, and where a higher standard of civilization has evolved, and is still evolving, than anywhere else. But this is not only concerning our own land. Today we are faced with the greatest organized challenge to Christianity and civilization that the world has ever seen, and I count myself lucky and honoured to be the right age and fully trained to throw my full weight into the scale. For this I have to thank you. Yet there is more work for you to do. The home front will still have to stand united for years after the war is won. For all that can be said against it, I still maintain that this war is a very good thing; every individual is having the chance to give and dare all for his principle like the martyrs of old. However long the time may be, one thing can never be altered — I shall have lived and died an Englishman. Nothing else matters one jot, nor can anything ever change it.

You must not grieve for me, for if you really believe in religion and all that it entails that would be hypocrisy. I have no fear of death; only a queer elation . . . I would have it no other way. The universe is so vast and so ageless that the life of one man can only be justified by the measure of his sacrifice. We are sent to this world to acquire a personality and a character to take with us that can never be taken from us. Those who just eat and sleep, prosper and procreate, are no better than animals if all their lives they are at peace.

I firmly and absolutely believe that evil things are sent into the world to try us; they are sent deliberately by our Creator to test our mettle because He knows what is good for us. The Bible is full of cases where the easy way out has been discarded for moral principles.

I count myself fortunate in that I have seen the whole country and known men of every calling. But with the final test of war I consider my character fully developed. Thus at my early age my earthly mission is already fulfilled and I am prepared to die with just one regret, and one only — that I could not devote myself to making your declining years more happy by being with you; but you will live in peace and freedom and I shall have directly contributed to that, so here again my life will not have been in vain.

Your loving Son.

131

WOODBINE WILLIE

(Geoffrey Studdert Kennedy 1883-1929)

He stood on an old ammunition box surrounded by a crowd of British soldiers in the early days of 1916, a small, black-frocked clergyman with a balding head and two of the biggest, saddest brown eyes that anybody in that company had ever seen. His "church" was a canteen beside a French railway station. But with a cigarette in his hand and a mischievous twinkle in his eye, he seemed more at home there than in an English pulpit on a Sunday morning.

To some church leaders back home in England, the Rev. Geoffrey Studdert Kennedy was an eccentric army chaplain with a braying laugh and a habit of forgetting to turn up for official duties (even funerals!). He was, in their view, a disruptive and unstable influence — but, like a Pied Piper, wherever he went ordinary people gathered to hear him speak, becoming completely spell-bound by his charm, humility and the clear message that he communicated.

The Reverend Geoffrey Anketell Studdert Kennedy, the man who was
known as "Woodbine Willie" to countless soldiers and victims of the
post-war Depression.

The British Tommies in that French canteen, waiting to board a train to take them to the Front, loved him too. He spoke in a language they could understand, sympathising with their doubts, but possessing an assurance that he somehow knew the truth of what he was saying. God, far from being indifferent, was involved in the sufferings of mankind — that was his message to all.

When he had finished speaking, the hoarse-voiced chaplain was ushered through the back-slapping crowd to an old piano. Here, with soldiers on every side, he sang an emotional repertoire of songs like *Mother Machree* and *The Sunshine of Your Smile*. Then, as the time drew near for the men to board the train, he moved amongst them shaking hands, looking at treasured photographs, and scribbling down names and addresses so that he could write to mothers, wives and sweethearts, letting them know he had seen their menfolk before they left for the Front. Their companion to the last, he followed them out to the train, walking along the outside and entering every carriage to present each man with a copy of the New Testament and — what became his legendary trademark — a packet of Wild Woodbine cigarettes. When he reached the end, the doors of the train were slammed shut and it started to pull away. The departing soldiers leaned out of the windows, waving and cheering to him. He returned their waves with a heavy heart, for he could see beyond their silhouettes to the distant horizon where the sky was awash with the red flames of battle.

Left alone, he walked back to the canteen. Only then did the doubts start to assail him — the same doubts that always followed this regular ritual of seeing the men off. How could he, a minister of God, justify a

system that sent so many men to die in this way? He could not know that very shortly he would be serving alongside those troops at the Front and that the nickname they gave him — "Woodbine Willie" — would outlast the war and become synonymous with all the affection and respect that the soldiers and people of post-war England felt for him.

"Woodbine Willie", the legendary padre and poet of the First World War, was born Geoffrey Anketell Studdert Kennedy on 27th June, 1883, one of eight children. His father was vicar of St. Mary's Church, Quarry Hill, a run-down district of Leeds. He attended Leeds Grammar School and while still in his teens made a vivid impression on all who met him, especially in the debating society which he would set alight with his arguments and speeches.

At home, Geoffrey's generosity was a frequent cause of amusement and not a little concern. If he met

MOTHER MACHREE (1).

There's a spot in me heart which no colleen may own,
There's a depth in me soul never sounded or known.
There's a place in my mem'ry, my life, that you fill,
No other can take it, no one ever will.

An old song-card depicting one of the lovely ballads Geoffrey used to sing to raise soldiers' spirits and remind them of home.

someone in the street who appeared to be less fortunate than himself, he thought nothing of giving away his coat or jacket. Similarly, just before the First World War when he was vicar of St. Paul's, Worcester, Geoffrey's new young wife, Emily, returned to their house one day to find her husband carting their bedstead on his back to the home of an invalid. Obviously accustomed to his ways, rather than complaining, she waited until his return and then helped him to take the mattress as well!

In January 1905, after completing his degree at Trinity College, Dublin, Geoffrey took up a teaching position at Calday Green in Cheshire. Then, after a short spell at Ripon Clergy College in Yorkshire, he was ordained deacon and went as curate to Rugby parish church. The year was 1909, and it was while he was there — and during his term as a curate in Leeds (1912-14) and vicar in Worcester (1914-15) which followed — that his reputation began to grow. He continued to give away what little money he had and actively sought out the poorest people. He became a familiar, welcome sight in the slums and unsavoury pubs, standing at the bar and singing songs, smoking, talking and joking with the men, and warming the coldest of hearts with his laughter and sunny smile.

His unorthodox methods were not, however, to everyone's liking. During a sermon in a church in straight-laced Rugby, where many of the stained glass windows had been placed in memory of friends and relations of members of the congregation, Geoffrey caused considerable consternation by declaring that he sometimes felt like smashing the stained glass with a sledge-hammer and conducting the service in the fields! Happily, whatever criticisms were levelled at this whirlwind, he never took offence, just as he was

Paradise

When machine-guns start to play
At the ending of the day,
And the sun's last burning ray
    Bleeds and dies.
When the sable warp of night
Is first cleft by silver light,
With its sudden curving flight
    Of surprise.
It is then that England calls
From its cottages and halls,
And we think of four dear walls
    And her eyes.
When the children's prayer is said,
And they lie tucked up in bed,
And the fire is burning red, —
    Paradise.

GEOFFREY STUDDERT KENNEDY

quick to forgive any personal slight to himself.

By the time Geoffrey became vicar of St. Paul's, Worcester, on 9th June, 1914, people were making a deliberate point of going to hear him speak. Many who witnessed his electrifying style — a torrent of words that the tender-hearted man seemed unable to stem — looked back on the experience as a watershed in their understanding of God. He could be preaching the most beautiful sermon inside an ancient church on a Sunday morning, and a few hours later be standing

Worcester Cathedral on the River Severn; the padre-poet and his wife lived in Worcester before and after the war.

Captured German trenches and the devasted Oosttaverne Wood after the Battle of Messines Ridge.

on a cold street corner addressing a crowd of cloth-capped workmen. He often liked to shock people to get a reaction, as on the occasion of an after-dinner speech to a group of Potteries businessmen. He stood up, surveyed the smartly dressed group, and with a wicked gleam in his eye exclaimed: "My God, but it's funny, the kind of people He allows to have money!"

Alcoholics, drug addicts and people with all sorts of problems confided in him, knowing full well that he would understand. Geoffrey, of course, did just that, his compassion often welling up into tears as he physically shared their pain and took their grief upon his own shoulders. When war was declared, he was as full of patriotic fervour as any man in England, believing in the rightness of the cause and eager to play a part. Even though he had only recently married, he volunteered and on 21st December, 1915, was appointed Temporary Chaplain to the Forces. For the first few months of 1916 he was at Rouen, tending to the welfare of the troops in that canteen and watching them depart with those famous cigarettes. In June 1916 he was posted to the Front as padre with the 157th Brigade of the 46th Division. Geoffrey was to experience two other periods in battle: in the following year with the 17th Brigade of the 24th Division, when he was involved in the attack on the Messines Ridge; and in the last year of the war when he took part in the final advance with the 42nd Division. It was during the

fighting at Messines that Geoffrey, under heavy fire, typically disregarded his own safety in order to tend his wounded comrades. For his gallantry and devotion to duty he was awarded the Military Cross.

Geoffrey had already started writing poetry and a collection of dialect verse entitled *Rough Rhymes* was published while he was still serving at the Front. The book was eagerly seized upon by the troops, for never had spiritual insights been presented in such a clear and

Lift Up Your Hearts

There are cowslips in the clearing,
With God's green and gold ablaze,
And the distant hills are nearing,
Through a sun-kissed sea of haze.

There's a lilt of silver laughter
In the brook upon its way,
With the sunbeams stumbling after
Like the children at their play.

There's a distant cuckoo calling
To the lark up in the sky
As his song comes falling, falling
To his nest — a happy sigh.

Sursum Corda! How the song swells
From the woods that smile and nod.
Sursum Corda! Ring the bluebells,
Lift up your hearts to God.

GEOFFREY STUDDERT KENNEDY

readable form. The chaplain's growing bitterness at the waste of war, as well as the way in which it tested his own faith and produced doubts and inner struggles, were explored further in two other books: *War Rhymes* and *Peace Rhymes*. The most frequent question put to Geoffrey was how could he *prove* the existence of God? To which he replied in the style of one of his street-corner discussions:

> *It isn't proved you fool, it can't be proved.*
> *How can you prove a victory before*
> *It's won? How can you prove a man who leads*
> *To be a leader worth following,*
> *Unless you follow to the death?*

Such was the depth of Geoffrey Studdert Kennedy's faith, achieved through tremendous thought and questioning. By the time the war ended the name of "Woodbine Willie" was known across the length and breadth of England and in the succeeding years of unemployment and hardship many people looked to him for inspiration and guidance. Geoffrey — now with two beloved sons, Christopher and Patrick, and soon to have another, Michael — was still vicar of St. Paul's, Worcester, but he was in great demand to speak all over the country, demands he felt unable to refuse. His speaking on behalf of the Life and Liberty Movement, a Church reform group, brought him into contact with two of the most important theologians of the day, Dick Sheppard and William Temple, both of whom remained good friends to the end of his life. Sheppard wrote a sparkling sketch of Geoffrey which brings the latter delightfully to life:

His laughter was a thing of joy, and his smile had a never-to-be-forgotten radiance. He would sit in an armchair, smoking endless cigarettes and drinking countless cups of tea, while he thrilled us with his wisdom and humour. To go to a theatre with him was to have your attention removed from the stage to the companion at your side, who was laughing with enjoyment. Then suddenly, at a touch of pathos in the play, those wonderful eyes would grow large and sad, and he was not ashamed of letting tears fall down his cheeks . . .

In 1922 Geoffrey was appointed to the living of St. Edmund's, Lombard Street in London, and he also accepted the post of chief missioner to the Industrial Christian Fellowship. So began an exhausting itinerary of pastoral duty in London which included many much talked about church services, brief dashing visits to his family who remained in Worcester, and a never-ending round of railway journeys from one end of the country to the other. The I.C.F. sought to take the gospels into the industrial cities and market places, so Geoffrey was shunted around from mission hall to street corner, from cathedral to church, talking to anyone and everyone who needed encouragement in those bleak years that bestrode the General Strike. Despite the terrible strain of it all, Geoffrey never lost his passionate enthusiasm. He was a driven man, intensely proud of the "Woodbine Willie" name and fiercely opposed to war and the social injustices of the time. His great ability to move the hearts and minds of men through speech remained undimmed, as the following report of a service on a Good Friday in London demonstrates:

On the stage, throughout the whole of the time, stood the priest, burning with nervous zeal. Men — there were hundreds of them — and women sat as if hypnotised, moved often to tears, held prisoner by the eloquence of

a man whose soul was on fire. The stage was at length, towards the end, invaded . . .

More often than not he would end close to tears himself, wracked by asthma and still unconvinced that he had done all he could. In between the interminable meetings and rallies, Geoffrey had also found the time to write several books — most notably *Food for the Fed Up, The Wicket Gate* and *The Word and the Work* which were an extension of his poems and talks in presenting religion in a manner comprehensible to the layman.

Overwork like this, of course, took its toll. During a visit to to Liverpool for a series of Lenten addresses Geoffrey was taken ill and died suddenly on 8th March, 1929, aged 45. It was a sadly premature death and one which, had he taken it easier, could have been avoided. But that was never the way of "Woodbine Willie". The solidity of his own faith had been formed

Liverpool, where Geoffrey died in 1929.

in conditions that most clergymen never have to experience. He had been forced to question his most basic beliefs in the hell-holes of the Somme and had been given certainty and strength. It was this terrible examination of his faith and its ultimate survival, stronger than ever, that drove him on and gave conviction to everything he said.

The achievement of Geoffrey Studdert Kennedy — the lives he touched and perhaps changed — cannot be measured in cold statistics. It is impossible to say who, after hearing him or reading him, took away something from the encounter that they had not had before.

Yet the way he was loved and listened to in those countless churches and halls shows that he must, indeed, have lit lights in people's souls that not even the Great War and industrial depression could extinguish. When the days were at their darkest and the established church seemed to offer no clear leadership or hope, Geoffrey Studdert Kennedy was a man who did — and all with deep humility, a sense of humour and a marvellous feeling for ordinary men and women.

That he had profoundly affected many people was demonstrated in the aftermath of his death, particularly in Liverpool and during the great funeral procession from Worcester Cathedral to St. John's cemetery. Shops were closed, crowds lined the streets and individuals from all walks of life came to pay their respects to this man of the people. One of the most abiding images was at Liverpool. The coffin was about to be put on the ferry for the first stage of its journey to Worcester, when an old man stepped out from the throng and placed something on the top. It was a packet of Woodbine cigarettes . . .

STEPHEN GARNETT

CHARLES SORLEY

(1895-1915)

There are 650 names carved on the wall of the Memorial Hall at Marlborough College in Wiltshire: unremarkable, easily forgettable names that could almost be part of the roll-call of present-day pupils and teachers. Try calling them out in the corridor, though, and not one of those young men will come running out of a nearby classroom. Stand on the touchline of the rugby field and shout with all your might over the buildings and across to the rolling downs. Only silence will greet your echoing voice. For those 650 are the names of the former pupils and masters of Marlborough College who alongside thousands of others, fell in foreign fields while fighting for their country during the two world wars. To read down that list of names when the school is full of life, laughter and hope, is to remember with renewed sadness all of the lives that were wasted and the bright futures that were so cruelly nipped in the bud.

One of the names on the memorial at Marlborough is that of Charles Hamilton Sorley, a pupil from 1908 to 1913, who was just beginning to flower into a great poet when his life was abruptly ended by a sniper's bullet near Loos on the Western Front in 1915. Like so many other brave young men of his generation, the place and manner of his death was in stark contrast to

Charles Hamilton Sorley, Autumn 1914.

the happy life he had led before the war Those years came to be looked back on with longing, as carefree, halcyon days.

For many people, of course, it was not such an idyllic time, but for Charles Sorley, the son of well-to-do parents and the recipient of a good education, it certainly seems to have been so, and he filled it with as much learning and simple enjoyment as he could. He began composing verse at a very early age, so that by the time he came to write his war poetry he was producing work of astonishing maturity.

Charles was born in Aberdeen on 19th May 1895, but when he was only five his father, William Ritchie Sorley, was awarded a professorship at Cambridge. This meant the whole family — Charles's mother, sister Jean and his twin brother Kenneth — moving to a

The Sorley children: Kenneth, Jean and Charles.

house which overlooked Magdalene College and the River Cam. After attending King's College Choir School as day boys, in 1908 the twins went their separate ways — Kenneth going to Westminster and Charles to Marlborough.

Going to live and work in Marlborough with its broad High Street, red-roofed houses and tempting tea-shops was a great adventure for Charles and he quickly settled into the rituals of public school life. A bright, outgoing boy, with a self-deprecating sense of humour and a sunny smile, he was well-liked by both masters and boys and made many friends. Sadly, a great number of them — like Herbert Ridley with whom he shared a study — were also fated to fall in the forthcoming war. Ridley went on to win the MC but was killed in action near Ypres in 1917.

Another school friend was Sidney Clayton Wood-roffe who fell on 30th July 1915 and was awarded a posthumous Victoria Cross. Charles Sorley wrote a simple and touching tribute to him, ironically only a few months before his own death:

> There is no fitter end than this.
> No need is now to yearn nor sigh,
> We know the glory that is his,
> A glory that can never die.
>
> Surely we knew it long before,
> Knew all along that he was made
> For a swift radiant morning, for
> A sacrificing swift night-shade.

One of Charles's favourite occupations at Marl-borough was cross–country running and although he was never happier than when with his friends, he also enjoyed making long, solitary walks to Liddington Castle and Aldbourne. These rambles through the countryside he loved were recalled in several of his poems. He was also deeply influenced by a number of writers, including Richard Jefferies, George Meredith, Thomas Hardy and John Masefield. He was a young man with an unquenchable zest for life and full of changing enthusiasms, literary heroes and interests.

It was his love of the outdoors more than anything else that led him, in 1910, to join the school's Officers' Training Corps. Always one for self-mockery, an incident that occurred when they were marching home and caused a horse to bolt, delighted him:

In a second we were all on the pavement, making for the wall; and we had been marching at attention under milit-ary discipline. I have never seen anything so disgraceful; but it just reminded us that we weren't all Wellingtons

The Wiltshire village of Aldbourne — a favourite haunt of the burgeoning young poet.

yet . . . . The humorous horse, when he saw us beginning to venture back into line again, settled down to a trot; and we marched back to bed trying hard to pretend it was a dream.

By the time he was 17 and in the sixth form, Charles was well-established at Marlborough and certainly one of the most active pupils there. He was a prefect, house captain, an entertaining member of the debating society and a regular contributor of papers to the

Charles, seated in the centre, with some of his Marlborough College classmates in 1912.

senior literary society. Nevertheless, he was also becoming something of a rebel and had begun to question both orthodox religion and the public school system. This was partly due to his growing desire to work for the underprivileged, but also because, as he became more popular, he was constantly afraid of becoming complacent, smug and self-satisfied. "One is awfully tempted," he wrote, "to pose all the time and be theatrical."

To avoid this pitfall and remain true to his feelings, after obtaining a scholarship to University College, Oxford, in 1913 he decided to leave Marlborough early — thus forgoing the two terms of leisure that he might have enjoyed. He went instead to Germany for six months, staying with a family to learn the language and attending a university there. He was very fond of

the people he met, so that when war was declared between Great Britain and Germany in the summer of
1914, he felt torn between the two.

Back in England he found the country gripped by
war fever, but despite his belief in the futility of war,
he did feel that he ought to fight. He volunteered
immediately and gained a commission with the seventh
battalion of The Suffolk Regiment. The same ambivalent attitude that he had felt at Marlborough continued
to torment him. While he was popular with the men
and enjoyed the feeling of doing something useful, he
was disturbed by the dulling effects of army life, his
position as an officer, and the danger that he might
become pompous and actually start enjoying it for its
own sake. Someone so honest, of course, was never
likely to lose sight of reality.

One of the last poems he wrote before leaving England captures the irony of the soldiers' situation, the
happy, jaunty rhythm contrasting powerfully with
the poem's message. This is the first verse:

> *All the hills and vales along*
> *Earth is bursting into song,*
> *And the singers are the chaps,*
> *Who are going to die perhaps.*
> *O sing, marching men,*
> *Till the valleys ring again.*
> *Give your gladness to earth's keeping,*
> *So be glad, when you are sleeping.*

The Suffolks arrived in France in May, 1915,
Charles and his men joining the frustrating stalemate
which increased his disillusionment. His thoughts
turned increasingly back to Marlborough and the
Downs, but also to the forthcoming action and a few
self-doubts about his own bravery. He need not have

Two Sonnets

Saints have adored the lofty soul of you.
Poets have whitened at your high renown.
We stand among the many millions who
Do hourly wait to pass your pathway down.
You, so familiar, once were strange: we tried
To live as of your presence unaware.
But now in every road on every side
We see your straight and steadfast signpost there.

I think it like that signpost in my land,
Hoary and tall, which pointed me to go
Upward, into the hills, on the right hand,
Where the mists swim and the winds shriek and blow,
A homeless land and friendless, but a land
I did not know and that I wished to know.

II

Such, such is Death: no triumph: no defeat:
Only an empty pail, a slate rubbed clean,
A merciful putting away of what has been.

And this we know: Death is not Life effete,
Life crushed, the broken pail. We who have seen
So marvellous things know well the end not yet.

Victor and vanquished are a-one in death:
Coward and brave: friend, foe. Ghosts do not say
'Come, what was your record when you drew breath?'
But a big blot has hid each yesterday
So poor, so manifestly incomplete.
And your bright Promise, withered long and sped,
Is touched, stirs, rises, opens and grows sweet
And blossoms and is you, when you are dead.

CHARLES SORLEY
12th June 1915

worried, for he proved his courage on several occasions and once — through his quick thinking when under fire — saved the lives of a couple of companions.

On 12th October Charles's commander was seriously wounded and he was sent for to secure the Company's defences. As he was adjusting a sandbag there was the sudden "ping" of a bullet and his head slumped quietly forward. No-one could believe that he was dead.

Charles Sorley was only 20 when he fell. His had been a brief, uneventful life, but one that had shown such tremendous promise for a future that would not now be. A modest, unassuming and good-humoured young man, he was also a gifted poet who, at a time when most other writers were proclaiming the glory of the war, could stand back and question it with chilling honesty. His final statement about the terrible tragedy of the war was found scribbled on a scrap of paper in his kit-bag:

When you see millions of the mouthless dead
Across your dreams in pale battalions go,
Say not soft things as other men have said,
That you'll remember. For you need not so.
Give them not praise. For, deaf, how should they know
It is not curses heaped on each gashed head?
Nor tears. Their blind eyes see not your tears flow.
Nor honour. It is easy to be dead.
Say only this, "They are dead." Then add thereto,
"Yet many a better one has died before."
Then, scanning all the o'ercrowded mass, should you
Perceive one face that you loved heretofore,
It is a spook. None wears the face you knew.
Great death has made all his for evermore.

STEPHEN GARNETT

157

Teach Me How To Die

This prayer was written during the Second World War by
Sergeant Hugh Brodie of the Royal Australian Air Force. He
was later reported "Missing from Operations".

Almighty and all present power,
Short is the prayer I make to Thee.
I do not ask in battle hour
For any shield to cover me.

The vast unutterable way,
From which the stars do not depart,
May not be turned aside to stay
The bullet flying to my heart.

I ask no help to strike my foe,
I seek no petty victory here,
The enemy I hate, I know,
To Thee, is also dear.

But this I pray, be at my side,
When death is drawing through the sky.
Almighty God, who also died,
Teach me the way I should die.

VJ DAY AT KHANBURI

On an August evening in 1945, Allied prisoners of war in the Japanese camp at Khanburi (Thailand) learned that, at last, the war was over and their terrible ordeal was finally at an end. Messengers went from one prison hut to another, calling out the occupants to hear the news by the light of oil lamps. But there were no demonstrations of happiness; the worn, tired faces reflected only shock and disbelief. Many sat in silence, some in tears, thanking God it was finished. Later that night the entire camp gathered in the darkness to sing forgotten and forbidden songs like "God Save the King", "Waltzing Matilda" and "The Star-Spangled Banner" until the small hours. Among them was an English army officer, John Durnford, who recorded the moment in this poem . . .

Educated at Sherborne School, Dorset, and Trinity Hall, Cambridge, John Durnford trained as a gunner and was commissioned in December 1940. He served with the Lanarkshire Yeomanry and was captured at the fall of Singapore in February 1942. After the war he returned to England and was given a Regular Commission.

"Gentlemen!" he said in tears, "the war is over",
Looking towards a yellow hurricane light,
Held up by someone in the struggling crowd,
I glimpsed your face, its usual smile
Checked in bewilderment at so much joy,
So you must once have looked when, as a boy,
They gave us gifts at Christmas — now, this Freedom.
Silent, the men sat on in darkness, bowed and still,
As though at prayers, or sleeping after death.
Then slowly, one by one, as a great crowd
Of ransomed spirits might attend their Lord,
Began impulsive movements towards the door.
Stars filled the jagged hills, the village slept.
The shuffling feet paused. Then someone sang,
Timid at first, their voices, gathered in strength,
Sounding a great hymn from the ragged lines,
While, all night long, drums beat in the darkened shrines.

F.W. Harvey in 1914 when he had enlisted in the Glosters.

F.W. HARVEY

(1888–1957)

If we return, will England be
Just England still to you and me?

For the man who wrote these lines in his poem *If We Return* just before going to fight in the First World War, England never was the same after 1918, and he spent the rest of his life trying to relive the past in the lanes and byways of his beloved Gloucestershire.

Frederick William Harvey was born in 1888 at Murrell's End in the little village of Hartpury. When he was two the family moved to Minsterworth, and it was here, on a farm named "The Redlands", that Will, as he was known by everyone, grew to love the quiet countryside of Gloucestershire that was to inspire his poetry all through his life.

Will's father, Howard, farmed with his brother Ernest, breeding shire-horses to pull plough and hay-wain, and also raising pigs, poultry and dairy cattle.

They were a familiar sight on market days in Gloucester and gained a reputation for honesty, kindness and hospitality. The Redlands was a favourite stopping place for friends and tramps alike, for no-one was ever turned away. Will's mother, Matilda, was his greatest friend. She taught him to play the piano, and he sought her comfort and guidance until the end of her life.

Short and stocky, Will described himself in a later poem as "A thick-set, dark-haired, dreamy little man, uncouth to see", but he had a great aptitude for learning and a marvellous memory — by the age of seven he could recite by heart all 330 lines of Robert Browning's *The Pied Piper of Hamelin*. He loved poetry and riding, and was an enthusiastic cricket, hockey and football player. Will also loved to spend hours alone in the rambling garden, or down by the duckpond, making up verses and studying Nature.

In 1897, at the age of nine, Will started at King's School in Gloucester, which provided choristers for

▷*Matilda, Will's mother and greatest friend.*

the cathedral. Although the headmaster was known for drunkenness and lack of discipline, and Will was soon transferred to Rossall School in Lancashire, he later claimed that he had learned to love music at Gloucester. At Rossall, Will won the school singing prize at the age of 16.

Leaving school in 1905, he did not know what he wanted to do with his life, so his mother took him to a phrenologist (someone who believes that a person's mental faculties can be discovered by feeling the bumps on the outside of his head), who pronounced that he was best suited to be either a musician or a lawyer, whereupon, the following year, Will found himself apprenticed to a Gloucester solicitor. In 1908, Will met another former pupil of King's School, Ivor Gurney who was now apprenticed to the Gloucester Cathedral organist, and thus began a lifelong friendship, filled with shared interests in music, poetry and Nature.

The Redlands, which remained in the poet's heart wherever he lived.

Although Will had been an enthusiastic participator in the church at Minsterworth, he had long been searching for a better way to express his love of God than in the Anglican Church, and his friend Pat Kerr started him thinking about Catholicism.

In 1911, Will failed his law exams and had to move to Lincoln's Inn Fields in London to cram for six months. While he was there, he attended the Brompton Oratory, then England's foremost Catholic church, and began receiving instruction in the Roman Catholic faith.

Will was still writing poetry but failing to get his work published. He began corresponding with the poet Lascelles Abercrombie, and was encouraged to continue writing by Ivor Gurney, himself a struggling poet. After qualifying as a solicitor, Will had surgery to remove a swollen gland in his neck, and fell in love with his nurse, Sarah Anne Kane, who was to become

The appalling conditions experienced by soldiers during the First World War are captured in this photograph showing troops on the Western Front in 1916.

his wife several years later. The terms of his articles of indenture prevented him from practising within 30 miles of Gloucester for 10 years, so Will was obliged to move to Chesterfield in Derbyshire. However, he was soon back in his beloved Gloucestershire to enlist in the county regiment at the beginning of the Great War.

Will's first taste of war was on the way to the front line trenches in Ploegsteert Wood. The ground was waterlogged and thick with mud, and the track through the wood was marked with sinking duck-boards. As Will's battalion passed through the blasted trees, searchlights suddenly swept the area followed by machine-gun bullets and rifle fire. Then, when they got to the end of the wood, they found no communication trenches, and had to dodge enemy bullets as they ran to the main trenches which were only 200 yards from the German front line.

Will spent three months in the muddy, rat-infested trenches, surrounded by ceaseless shelling and gunfire. Yet he managed to make light of the situation in his contributions to the *Fifth Gloucester Gazette*, one of the first trench magazines to be published in France. One of these regular features was "Nature Notes", in which he once commented, "Quite a feast of song is afforded by the nightingales in the vicinity of our trenches".

In 1915 Will was awarded the Distinguished Conduct Medal and recommended for a commission for helping to take a German listening post in No Man's Land. Afterwards, Ivor Gurney reported to friends that Will was "pretty shaky" about having killed someone in hand-to-hand combat.

Before taking up his commission, Will was given leave and returned home. He was amazed that most people were so ignorant about conditions at the Front and still believed the war to be a wonderful adventure. He expressed his disgust in the *Gazette* upon his return to France: "Oh, yes, I like shelling. It is a glorious and exhilarating sensation. Any of the London daily papers will tell you so."

Finally, in 1916, Will managed to get his first book of poems published by Sidgwick and Jackson, who had also published Rupert Brooke's work. *A Gloucestershire Lad* became an immediate success, especially

A Rondel of Gloucestershire

Big glory mellowing on the mellowing hills,
And in the little valleys, thatch and dreams,
Wrought by the manifold and vagrant wills
Of sun and ripening rain and wind; so gleams
My country, that great magic cup which spills
Into my mind a thousand thousand streams
Of glory mellowing on the mellowing hills
And in the little valleys, thatch and dreams.

O you dear heights of blue no ploughman tills,
O valleys where the curling mist upsteams
White over fields of trembling daffodils,
And you old dusty little water-mills,
Through all my life, for joy of you, sweet thrills
Shook me, and in my death at last there beams
Big glory mellowing on the mellowing hills
And in the little valleys, thatch and dreams.

F.W. HARVEY

Will (centre, with beard), in captivity at Holzminden.

as its author had just been reported missing in action. Though no-one at home realised it, Will had only been captured, not killed. He had been in the trenches at Laventie, when he decided to explore the area he was to patrol that night. No-one seemed to be around, and he worked his way across No Man's Land and into a German trench without being seen. However, he was eventually trapped in the trench and taken prisoner.

"It is a strange thing, but to be made prisoner is undoubtedly the most surprising thing that can happen to a soldier", he wrote later. His first reaction was to laugh, but when he was put into a tiny cell after being questioned, the reality struck home.

"By God", I spoke suddenly to the room, "they've got me!" Everything — room, lice, solitude, dirty black bread, bowl of disgusting brown soup — corroborated that statement. I was a prisoner. I should be reported missing. My mother would be duly notified, and would grieve, not knowing whether I was alive or dead. My friends in the regiment would go out to look for me. Possibly they would get killed searching. It was horrible — horrible.

Will was taken first to the Gütersloh prisoner-of-war camp where, in order to overcome the frustration and boredom, he amused himself and everyone else by acting in home-made plays, contributing to the camp newspapers, singing and taking part in sports. His nickname changed from "The Little Man" to "The Poet", and he wrote later that "I know that never again in this life shall I hold so high and happy a position amid my fellows".

Will became active in a tunnel-digging party, but the tunnel had to be abandoned a few yards short of completion when the British prisoners were transferred. The agonising decision was made by the officers in charge not to try and escape through the tunnel, but to leave it as a contribution for the "Cause".

In 1917, Will was able to get a selection of poems sent back to England, which was published under the

If We Return

If we return, will England be
Just England still to you and me?
The place where we must earn our bread?
We, who have walked among the dead,
And watched the smile of agony.
And seen the price of Liberty
Which we have taken carelessly
From other hands. Nay, we shall dread,
    If we return.

Dread lest we behold blood-guiltily
The things that men have died to free.
Oh, English fields shall blossom red
For all the blood that has been shed
By men whose guardians are we,
    If we return.

F.W. HARVEY

title *Gloucestershire Friends*. He then went through a succession of camps, trying to keep up his spirits and write despite frustration and depression. On the way to Holzminden, 30 miles south of Hanover, he jumped from a train, but was recaptured with the help of suspicious villagers and accused of being a spy — one of the reasons being that the authorities thought the large, hard camp biscuits in his pack were slabs of dynamite to blow up a railway tunnel!

At Holzminden, Will was put into a cell and forced to stay there with little exercise and no fresh air. He couldn't write, grew despondent, and neglected his personal appearance. He collected lists of words from a dictionary and used these to fashion poems later on. One flash of inspiration amid the gloom came from a chalk drawing on the wall of ducks on a pond. They

The Gloucester Hockey Club in 1921. Will Harvey is on the far right of the picture.

reminded him of Minsterworth and inspired his famous poem, *Ducks*.

When he was finally repatriated Will was immediately sent to Leeuwarden in Holland to help distribute food and clothing to returning troops. Then he had to help feed Italians and Portuguese soldiers at Harderwijk, and was not sent home until he caught Spanish flu in 1919.

Back home, Will was changed. He still enjoyed Nature whilst he worked as a solicitor, but was frustrated at the living conditions of the country. He had thought that he and his fellow soldiers had suffered in Europe in order to build a better world in England, but things had, if anything, become worse. There was still abject poverty and corruption, and Will became a staunch advocate for the lower classes, even though his clients could seldom afford to pay him. Meanwhile, he struggled on with his poetry, trying to create work that would be enjoyed by ordinary people, as

well as pieces that reflected his deep personal emotions. He believed that a closeness with Nature was the key to true art ("You will never enjoy the world aright", he wrote, "till the sea itself floweth in your veins").

But though the public enjoyed his books, he was not satisfied that he was expressing himself properly. In 1921 he even contemplated giving up poetry in order to concentrate on earning a living as a solicitor so he could raise a family with his new wife, Sarah Anne Kane.

His book *September and Other Poems*, published in 1925, was filled with the disillusionment that was to mar his later years.

My dreams? They flee.
Discomforted.
I am dead,
Less than alone
Less than a worm, a tree,
A stone.

He longed for the companionship of the war years, when he had felt truly alive, and even having his work included in the prestigious *Augustan Book of Poetry* series, which marked his acceptance as a major British poet, did not make him feel useful. Moving deeper into Gloucestershire's Forest of Dean, he became a familiar figure in the local inns and lanes. Children would stop him in the street and ask for a poem, and he would recite Shakespeare and Milton in the pubs. By now, he was carelessly dressed, bearded and a heavy drinker, and his legal practice was declining. And when the Second World War began, he saw it as a betrayal by the politicians of everything he had worked for during the Great War.

In 1956, Will was taken to Gloucester to hear once again that stirring oratorio *The Dream of Gerontius*, which had inspired his faith at the beginning of his life. Shortly afterwards, he fell ill and took to his bed. His last words to his friend Brian Frith were "I have burnt myself out for Gloucestershire". He died on 13th February, 1957.

Although he was known during his lifetime as "The Laureate of Gloucestershire", perhaps Will Harvey's philosophy is best summed up in his own words, taken from his poem *F. W.H., a Portrait*, and which are inscribed on his memorial tablet, in Gloucester Cathedral, unveiled in 1980:

"He loved the vision of this world and found it good."

LYNN PARR

KEITH DOUGLAS

(1920–1944)

The night of the 23rd October 1942 was humid and still, with shafts of moonlight casting silver shadows over the golden dunes of the Western Desert. Suddenly, the silence was broken by the boom of heavy guns and the dusky sky erupted with brilliant flashes as the full might of the Eighth Army was unleashed against Rommel. The Battle of El Alamein had begun.

The noise was so intense that it reached 20 miles behind the lines to a young soldier serving as a camouflage officer. Like so many young men fighting for their country, he had an overwhelming desire to be part of the battle — a desire which overcame his natural apprehension of what might befall him and the conviction that he would never see the end of the war. For four days he tried desperately to ignore the sounds of the battle, but then he had had enough. Putting on a freshly-laundered uniform, he "borrowed" a truck and drove off at full pelt for the Front to join his regiment. He was a soldier — a man who wanted to fight and, if necessary, die for King and Country.

Yet this same soldier was also the kind of man who, a year later while training for the invasion of Europe,

Keith Douglas in the desert, 1942.

could forget the war so completely that he ordered his men to go out into the woods on an English spring morning — and pick primroses! All the huts of the army encampment were soon full of bunches of flowers crammed into any available can or pot and their freshness and scent banished for a time the grim reality of the imminent battle. For above all, this soldier was a poet who, though full of manly instincts, had an eye for beauty and truth. Although wanting to fight he was also deeply aware of the horror and bestiality of

Keith, at the age of 10, in his garden wigwam.

war, and such a combination made Keith Douglas one of the greatest soldier poets of the Second World War.

Keith Castellain Douglas, born on 24th January, 1920, in the Regency spa town of Tunbridge Wells, Kent, was the son of Marie Josephine and Captain Keith Sholto Douglas, MC. His father had left the Army in 1919, and later became a chicken farmer in Cranleigh, Surrey. Like most small boys, Keith loved nothing better than to parade around the house with his toy gun and pudding-basin helmet pretending to be a soldier. He avidly listened to stories of his father's exploits in the Army.

The chicken farm was quite successful until 1924 when Mrs. Douglas became seriously ill with a form of sleeping sickness. Although now virtually unknown, this illness was common after the First World War and though rarely fatal, sufferers were ill for months, and even years later were plagued with headaches, amnesia and lack of concentration. The long illness and the

Artists at work in the Pantiles, Royal Tunbridge Wells. Keith Douglas was born in the town in 1920.

hospital fees proved a severe financial burden to the family until, finally, the farm had to be sold and Captain Douglas left home to look for work.

In September 1926, with a loan from a family friend, young Keith Douglas was sent to board at Edgeborough School in Guildford, Surrey. Even at the age of six his literary abilities were obvious — he enjoyed writing stories and even bought himself a dictionary of synonyms at Woolworth's, so that he wouldn't have to use the same word twice! At Edgeborough he did very well both academically and on the sporting field and was one of those gifted children who excel at everything — a strong, good-looking boy who made friends easily. However, when he realised that his father's absence from home was going to be permanent and that his parents' marriage had broken down, he became moody and difficult. His mother had financial problems to contend with as well as recurring bouts of sickness and she had to move frequently, either staying with friends or working as a hired help.

Keith's lack of security made him rebellious and resentful of authority and yet he was so talented that in 1931 he was able to win a place at Christ's Hospital School, near Horsham in Sussex. This famous public school, which was founded in 1552 as a royal charitable foundation, took a certain percentage of its scholars from elementary schools in the London area. It originally educated motherless and fatherless children and even today 80% of its pupils have their fees paid for by the foundation. The scholars wear a distinctive uniform of long blue coat with knee breeches and yellow stockings. Keith began writing poetry for pleasure and much of his work was published in the school magazine *The Outlook*. He could have enjoyed his success and popularity, but instead some deep hidden feeling that life was too easy made him argumentative and rebellious to such an extent that he was nearly expelled.

Surprisingly, despite his loathing for all forms of authority, Keith thoroughly enjoyed the school's Officer Training Corps. He was a model soldier who loved drilling and kept his uniform immaculately clean and his boots sparkling — yet in civilian life he was sloppy and untidy! His hard-working mother had bought a bungalow in Bexhill-on-Sea, Sussex, which she rented out during the holiday season, but although this provided her and Keith with much-needed income, it did mean that when school broke up for the holidays he had no home to go to and had to stay with

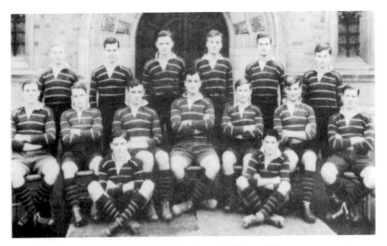

The First XV at Christ's Hospital School, Sussex.
Keith is seated second from the right.

friends. This nomadic life affected him and, although he had all his mother's love, he suffered the lack of a father's guiding hand. He felt embittered by the desertion of his father, whom he had not heard from since 1928. When ten years later his father wrote suggesting they meet, it was too late. The breach was past healing and they were never to see each other again. In 1938 Keith won an open scholarship to Merton College, Oxford, and he left Christ's in a blaze of triumph winning school prizes and colours for swimming and rugby.

Despite the threatening murmurs of war, Oxford was a paradise for Keith. Free from rules and regulations he revelled in his new life, cutting quite a dash in university circles with his flamboyant style of dressing. In his tweed hacking-jacket and bright yellow tie decorated with foxes' masks, he looked quite the English country gentleman. He was also privileged to have the poet Edmund Blunden as his tutor, who recognised Keith's enormous talents. Keith spent most of his time writing articles and poetry for the university

A bird's-eye view over the roof-tops and towers of Oxford.

magazine *The Cherwell*, eventually co-editing this famous weekly with my father, David Beaty. In fact Keith devoted so much of his time to *The Cherwell* that Blunden accepted his article in the magazine as his weekly essay.

The university OTC also took up much of Keith's time and my father remembers that the very different sides of his character were rather summed up by his favourite records. Echoing round the quadrangle from Keith's rooms would come either Haydn's Military Symphony — or "Jeepers, Creepers, where d'ye get those peepers?"

Keith led a full and enjoyable social life at Oxford, falling in love with (among others) the daughter of the one-time Chinese ambassador to Washington. Betty Sze (Yingcheng) was an elegant and sophisticated Oxford undergraduate who had come up from Cheltenham Ladies' College. Although they did become engaged, the relationship was not to last and Keith was desolated. However, he soon found another girl friend and when he quickly became engaged once more, his mother was understandably concerned! Because of the threat of war, and his own unsettled background, he was desperately searching for someone to love. With all the uncertainties of what lay ahead, and consumed by a conviction that he would not return, Keith needed a sweetheart. As he reveals in his letters, he needed a reason to fight "for the chance of a life worth living afterwards".

With typical defiance, when war was declared he flouted the university warning that undergraduates should wait before enlisting, though he was not called up until July 1940. Before he left Oxford he gave all his poetry to Edmund Blunden in the hope that he could find a publisher for it.

Keith was sent to Edinburgh with the Third Horsed Cavalry Training Regiment. He was quite at home in the saddle, having learnt to ride whilst staying with friends, and he liked being with horses. When Keith moved on to the Royal Military College, Sandhurst, he was persuaded to change to a tank regiment, having been assured that he would soon learn to love his tank as much as his horse. He passed out from Sandhurst in February 1941 and joined the 2nd Derbyshire Yeomanry at Ripon, Yorkshire. His intensive training programme left him little time to write poetry, but he did receive encouraging praise from T.S. Eliot who had been sent copies of his poems by Edmund Blunden.

Eventually, in July 1941, Keith was posted to the Nottinghamshire (Sherwood Rangers) Yeomanry who were waiting to be mechanised in Palestine. Keith

found the waiting frustrating and when Tobruk was relieved he was convinced that he would not get a chance to see action. Instead he was appointed as a camouflage staff officer to the 10th Armoured Division in Palestine. It was an excellent job and the living conditions were luxurious compared with living in tents in the desert. Keith also enjoyed a hectic social life with no shortage of girl friends, as the ladies found his good looks and confident manner an irresistible combination!

Meanwhile, the Sherwood Rangers had left to take up positions for the forthcoming confrontation with Rommel. When the Battle of El Alamein began, Keith could have remained in relative comfort and security some distance behind the lines. Instead, as at school, he couldn't bear the easy option — he wanted a life fraught with danger and excitement even if it cost him his life, and so he risked a Court Martial by making his unauthorised headlong flight to the Front. When he

The Creator

The unwearied sun from day to day,
along his mathematic way
looks with an infant's eyes upon
what little in the world's not wrong;
and with no understanding tear
at the death of a sad year.

So he forgets and turns away west,
while with fine uninterest
and in bone idle groups the stars
stupidly linger, and watch pass
erupting woe and queasy mirth
across the sallow face of earth.

And surely God, with never less
ignorance of pity or remorse,
is gaping at the eternal course
of sorrow, all His planning. Yes,
He's petrified and cannot see
His marvellous inefficiency.

KEITH DOUGLAS

arrived, the Sherwood Rangers were too involved with the fighting to question his unexpected appearance in their midst, and Keith soon found himself in charge of a tank, and in the forefront of the action.

Instead of dealing a death-blow to Rommel, as they had expected, the Sherwood Rangers found they were fighting a skilful and ruthless enemy and their losses were high. Rommel had been ordered by Hitler not to

Montgomery, who was the Army Commander at El Alamein, pictured with Winston Churchill.

retreat and the Rangers found themselves pinned down by heavy gunfire. At one time Keith found himself in the leading tank of the Eighth Army, as he drove it in much the same reckless style as he did everything else. He hated conforming to the rules and his habit of leaping out of the tank and hurling hand grenades at the enemy earned him a rebuke that he should leave the "Cowboy and Indian stuff" to the infantry! However, his courage and sense of humour won him the affection and admiration of the Sherwood Rangers. The advance against the enemy was slow and made with great loss of life — only six of the regiment's 22 officers came out unscathed. Finally, on 11th November 1942, they heard the church bells of England ring out on their radio to proclaim their hard-won victory at El Alamein.

Now that, for a time, the fighting was over, the authorities caught up with Keith and he was summoned to headquarters. His colonel interceded on his behalf and he was allowed back to his regiment after apologising for his behaviour. The final part of the North African campaign was now under way and the Sherwood Rangers joined other troops to engage the enemy. In the midst of the fighting Keith's tank was immobilised by gunfire and he was forced to retreat on foot. Unluckily, he walked through a mine-field, and spent six weeks in hospital at El Ballah in Egypt recovering from his wounds. When he was fit enough to return, he started to write down his battle experiences in a diary and these were published after the war, *Alamein to Zem Zem* (1946). He also wrote about his feelings towards those he fought with and against:

"It is exciting and amazing to see thousands of men, very few of whom have much idea why they are fighting, all enduring hardships, living in an unnatural, dangerous, but not wholly terrible world, having to kill and be killed, and yet at intervals moved by a feeling of comradeship with the men who kill them and whom they kill, because they are enduring and experiencing the same things. It is tremendously illogical — to read about it cannot convey the impression of having walked through the looking-glass which touches a man entering battle".

In early 1943 some of Keith's poems had appeared in *Selected Poems* by J.C. Hall and he had been offered a job in military journalism. Now promoted to Captain, he again refused a comfortable occupation and preferred to remain with his regiment. When on 7th November, 1943, the Sherwood Rangers were told to remove their cap badges and flashes for a secret destination, they knew they were coming back home to England to train for the invasion of Europe. While on leave, Keith was able to visit friends in Oxford and Cornwall and spend time with his much-loved mother. In his poem "Sanctuary", Keith expresses what a support she had been to him:

Once my mother was a wall;
behind my rampart and my keep
in a safe and hungry house
I lay as snug as a winter mouse:
till the wall breaks and I weep
for simple reasons first of all.

There then followed a period of intense training in preparation for the landings in Normandy. Thousands of troops poured into Southern England ready to attack the enemy. No-one knew when the call would come, and Keith waited with his regiment in the

lovely Hampshire village of Sway, nestling in the gorse and heather-covered sward of the New Forest. On the Sunday before they were due to leave for France Keith received Communion with others of his regiment at a hastily erected altar beside his tank. Later that evening, as the regimental padre took Evensong at the local parish church, he was surprised to see a soldier present. Keith Douglas was not a church-goer, but facing what he felt would be his certain death, he wanted to make his peace with God. After the service he talked with the padre for many hours as they walked through the Forest, parting only as dawn broke.

At midnight on the 5th June, 1944, the invasion of Europe began and Keith was a part of one of the most extraordinary armadas the world has ever known. The barges carrying troops and weapons were protected by an iron wall of warships and anti-U-boat bombers formed a huge screen around them. It was an amazing and spectacular arrival and Keith fought as hard and courageously as every other soldier on that momentous day.

Four days later, after returning to camp from patrol, his tank came under mortar attack. Leaping out of it, Keith dived for cover into a nearby ditch just as a shell exploded above him. He was killed instantly, though there was no mark on his body.

Keith Douglas lost his life as a soldier but as poet he will always live on. His poetry is as strong and defiant as he was in personality — he can portray powerful and painful images that shock the reader and yet at other times he can soothe the soul. In him the conflicting interests of soldier and poet vied with each other for dominance, but it was as a poet that he wanted to be remembered. The triumph and the tragedy of his life was that he gave us poetry of such quality, and yet there was still such a huge store of undreamt wealth within him. While with my father at Oxford, Keith had pointed to the memorial for the First World War and said, with a chilling conviction, that his name would soon be inscribed there, among those who died in the Second World War. And he left his own strange requiem:

> And all my endeavours are unlucky explorers
> come back, abandoning the expedition,
> the specimens, the lilies of ambition
> still spring in their climate, still unpicked;
> but time, time is all I lacked
> to find them, as the great collectors before me.

SUSAN BEATY

The following verses were written for the New Year of 1916 by Lieutenant Herbert Asquith, second son of the Prime Minister, Herbert Henry Asquith, who served at Downing Street from 1908 until December 1916. It is one of the most poignant poems of the period.

The Old New Year

The Old Year goes with all its vanished flow'rs;
  Across the fields we hear the distant bells;
To other music fade the dying hours,
  Leaving a heritage of long farewells.
What world is this, to which the New Year comes?
  A world by God forgotten, lost to Man?
A weary battlefield of broken homes,
  A red monotony without a plan?

No! Love and Laughter live; and Chivalry
  Still holds the seas from sunset to the dawn;
The sacred wells of Honour are not dry,
  And still for her the brightest blades are drawn!
The young Crusaders go to battle singing,
  And we, who listen to that song, may know,
Again the bells of Freedom will be ringing,
  As they were rung a hundred years ago.

With only his thoughts for company, an old soldier at Ironbridge in Shropshire remembers his fallen comrades.

Lament

We who are left, how shall we look again
Happily on the sun, or feel the rain,
Without remembering how they who went
Ungrudgingly, and spent
Their all for us, loved, too, the sun and rain?

A bird among the rain-wet lilac sings—
But we, how shall we turn to little things
And listen to the birds and winds and streams
Made holy by their dreams,
Nor feel the heart-break in the heart of things?

WILFRID GIBSON

Edward Thomas in 1913, when all of his poetry was still to be written.

190

EDWARD THOMAS

(1878-1917)

S pring came to England in 1917 just as bright and beautiful as it had ever done before. The daffodils were golden on the edges of green woodland and amongst the wild hedgerows of quiet country lanes; cuckoos sang and church bells chimed, sending their lovely music soaring across farmers' fields where seeds were being patiently sown; and the skies were as blue as thrushes' eggs, dappled here and there with wisps of white cloud. But all was not quite the same. England was still at war and there wasn't a family in the land that tragedy had not touched in some way by the loss of a dear father, son or friend. The sadness of it all was captured by a poet of the time in four heart-rending lines:

The flowers left thick at nightfall in the wood
This Eastertide call into mind the men,
Now far from home, who, with their sweethearts, should
Have gathered them and will do never again.

The author of this short poem was Edward Thomas who was himself serving at the Front with the Royal Garrison Artillery. All too predictably, he was one of those many thousands of brave men who were destined never to return to the England that they loved. Aged 39, he was killed at Arras just over 70 years ago on Easter Monday (9th April) 1917, leaving behind Helen his devoted wife, three children, a great gulf in the lives of his close friends, and a small collection of poems that are amongst the finest pieces of country verse ever written.

Today it is these poems for which Edward Thomas is best remembered, ensuring him a reputation that has continued to grow. Nevertheless, these 144 poems were nearly never written at all. They came right at the end of his life, poured out at a startling, white-hot pace in the space of just two years. The rest of his literary career had been an unrewarding treadmill of innumerable articles, book reviews and other prose works, written, more often than not, to keep the wolf from his family's door. It was only his passion for the English countryside that drove him on and made the bursting forth of his poems so irresistible; the same passion that led him to that fateful moment at Arras when a shell exploded, killing him instantly. He need not have been there, fighting for his country, at all. Much easier and safer options had presented themselves to him. But Edward Thomas was not a man to sidestep what he believed he had to do, however hard. He was not that sort of man at all . . .

Philip Edward Thomas was born on 3rd March 1878 at Lambeth in London, the eldest son (there would be six boys in all) of a loving mother and a stiff, rather self-righteous father who held a secure and respectable position at the Board of Trade. His plans were for Edward to follow him into the Civil Service, an ambition that in time caused bitter disagreement between the two.

Edward's childhood was a happy one, highlighted by Nature rambles on the local commons and visits to Wiltshire, the beautiful land of his great literary hero

Edward Thomas moved around a great deal during his life and lived in many different places. On the right can be seen the house in Battersea where he lived for a short time.

Richard Jefferies. He romanticised rural life and loved to talk with an old countryman, "Dad" Uzzell, whom he first met one day while walking in the fields between Swindon and Wootton Bassett. He learnt all about natural history, folklore and country ways from "Dad" and later immortalised him in one of his most popular poems, "Lob".

In 1894 Edward was attending St. Paul's School where he first began writing about his country experiences. He became a frequent visitor to the home of a well-known literary critic, James Ashcroft Noble, who encouraged him with his writing. Edward's first book *The Woodland Life* was published in 1897. He also became very friendly with Noble's daughter Helen and soon the two were deeply in love, despite Mrs. Noble's opposition to the romance. These were golden, carefree days for Edward and Helen, and they went on many walks and picnics together. Helen described the warmth of her feelings for Edward when they met to spend a day on Wimbledon Common:

> He was there waiting for me, so tall, so distinguished from other men, dressed as always with a sort of carelessness that was not at all untidy, but just easy and individual . . . No lover could have pleased the eye more, no girl have been prouder of her man than I of mine, and the wonder of his loving me never left me . . .

In March 1898 Edward began studying history at Lincoln College, Oxford. He continued to write, anxious eventually to make a living with his pen. Shy and inclined to melancholy and self-doubt, he nevertheless entered into the busy life of the college — even rowing for them.

Edward and Helen were married at Fulham Registry Office on 20th June 1899. Their son Merfyn was born at the beginning of the following year. Responsibilities were suddenly crowding in upon Edward and he became increasingly worried about how he could support his family. He was bitterly disappointed with his second-class degree but was still fiercely determined to earn his living by writing. Helen, of course, supported him in everything, but there ensued a blazing row with Mr. Thomas who was scornful of his son's ideals and ambitions. Writing was all very well, sneered Mr. Thomas, but it wasn't a profession you could make a living from. Edward steadfastly refused to try for a post in the Civil Service and the resulting rift between them was never completely healed.

Having made his decision Edward now faced the penurious existence of the freelance writer. From their dingy lodgings in London Edward was forced to tramp between newspaper offices in search of commissions, a pattern that was to continue right up to his

Helen Thomas in 1898, aged 21.

enlistment in 1915. He became a regular contributor to the *Daily Chronicle*, but on the whole the availability of work was patchy and he was always underpaid, with little time to write what he wanted. He frequently read five or six books a day, working into the small hours and receiving only a pittance at the end of it all. The tragedy of it was that he was incapable of doing a shoddy job and devoted precious time and talent to everything he did. When work was not forthcoming he often had to sell some of his own beloved books so that bills could be paid; the result of it all, exhaustion, depression and his occasional cutting remarks towards poor Helen which later filled him with remorse.

But there were happy times, too, especially when they moved out of London and lived in the countryside of Kent and then Hampshire. In October 1902, while they were living in the village of Bearsted, their second child Bronwen was born. Later on in his life, Edward wrote an affectionate series of "household poems" to his wife and each of their three children (a second daughter, Myfanwy, was born in 1910). In the lines to Bronwen he listed with relish some of the quaint old Essex place-names:

If I should ever by chance grow rich
I'll buy Codham, Cockridden, and Childerditch,
Roses, Pyrgo, and Lapwater —
And let them all to my elder daughter.
The rent I shall ask of her will be only
Each year's first violets, white and lonely,
The first primroses and orchises —
She must find them before I do, that is.
But if she finds a blossom on furze
Without rent they shall all for ever be hers,
Codham, Cockridden, and Childerditch,
Roses, Pyrgo, and Lapwater —
I shall give them all to my elder daughter.

A lovely portrait of Edward Thomas in 1900 with his son Merfyn.

Around this time Edward was given the first of his many book commissions — a 60,000-word volume about Oxford for which he was paid £100. Welcome as this was, it was hard earned, for the book had to be completed in four months and it depressed Edward terribly that he could not spend more time on it and

Edward with daughter Myfanwy and a neighbour's son.

make it into a first-class work. He was faced with this soul-destroying state of affairs with nearly every book he wrote, and ended up exhausted and quite often despising what he had written.

Edward and Helen moved house regularly, seeing each change as a new beginning, an excuse for fresh hope and, perhaps, a step nearer the attainment of those wild dreams they had had during their courting days and which no amount of hardship could crush. By the middle of 1904 they were ensconced in Else Farm near Sevenoaks in the picturesque Weald of Kent. Worn out though he might be, Edward was

Lights Out

I have come to the borders of sleep,
The unfathomable deep
Forest, where all must lose
Their way, however straight
Or winding, soon or late;
They can not choose.

Many a road and track
That since the dawn's first crack
Up to the forest brink
Deceived the travellers,
Suddenly now blurs,
And in they sink.

Here love ends —
Despair, ambition ends;
All pleasure and all trouble,
Although most sweet or bitter,
Here ends, in sleep that is sweeter
Than tasks most noble.

There is not any book
Or face of dearest look
That I would not turn from now
To go into the unknown
I must enter, and leave, alone,
I know not how.

The tall forest towers:
Its cloudy foliage lowers
Ahead, shelf above shelf:
Its silence I hear and obey
That I may lose my way
And myself.

EDWARD THOMAS

A horse-rider clip-clops along the Pilgrims' Way from Wrotham to Canterbury in the Weald of Kent. Edward Thomas tramped this part of the country many times.

beginning to make a name for himself as a reviewer and literary critic. On his visits to London he would go to a favourite restaurant to meet his old Oxford cronies and also many of the poets and writers whose works he had helped to popularise, including Arthur Ransome, Walter de la Mare, John Drinkwater and W.H. Davies, all of whom became his friends. Edward was a handsome figure in his country clothes, with piercing blue eyes, fair hair and a healthy, ripe sun tan. Those friends and fellow writers liked him enormously for his honesty, simplicity and humour. Walter de la Mare has left a delightful picture of him:

> The smile was whimsical, stealthy, shy, ardent, mocking, ironical by turns . . . The voice was low and monotonous, with a curious sweetness and hollowness when he sang his old Welsh songs to his children . . . What he gave to a friend in his company was not only himself, but that friend's self made infinitely less clumsy and shallow than usual, and at ease . . . Nobody like him was in this world that I have ever had the happiness to meet; others of his friends have said the same.

At home Edward was no different, finding immense joy in the ordinary things of life. Walking, fishing and planting flowers and trees in their garden were among his greatest pleasures, as were helping the local farmer with his harvest, skilfully making tables, chairs, and shelves for the cottage, and watching — usually with a child on his shoulders — the local blacksmith or wheelwright practising his craft. Times might be hard financially and the worries and frustrations sometimes too much to bear, but he was never scared of spending his last pound to buy a gift for Helen, or waking the whole family at dawn to take them on an adventurous fishing expedition.

During the next few years as he wrote books about Richard Jefferies and George Borrow, and researched for his *In Pursuit of Spring* and *The South Country*, there was hardly a lane or byway in Somerset, Wiltshire and the south of England that had not heard the crunch of his striding feet; hardly a gate or stile that had not borne his weight as he rested a while, puffing on his old clay pipe. The family moved again — first to Ashford in Hampshire and then to Petersfield and the village of Steep.

The American poet Robert Frost who became a close friend of Edward and Helen.

Edward Thomas counted many poets and writers among his acquaintances, including Rupert Brooke, W.H. Hudson, Hilaire Belloc and Eleanor Farjeon. His greatest friend, though, was the American Robert Frost to whom he was introduced in October 1913. Edward and Helen spent some wonderfully idyllic days with him at Leadington, the corner of Gloucestershire that had become a focus for a number of poets. They drank cider together, sang folk songs in the pubs and, most importantly, talked about poetry. It was

The Green Roads

The green roads that end in the forest
Are strewn with white goose feathers this June,

Like marks left behind by someone gone to the forest
To show his track. But he has never come back.

Down each green road a cottage looks at the forest.
Round one the nettle towers; two are bathed in flowers.

An old man along the green road to the forest
Strays from one, from another a child alone.

In the thicket bordering the forest,
All day long a thrush twiddles his song.

It is old, but the trees are young in the forest,
All but one like a castle keep, in the middle deep.

That oak saw the ages pass in the forest:
They were a host, but their memories are lost,

For the tree is dead: all things forget the forest
Excepting perhaps me, when now I see

The old man, the child, the goose feathers at the edge of
the forest,
And hear all day long the thrush repeat his song.

EDWARD THOMAS

Edward (second from left, middle row) and comrades in 1915.

due to Frost's encouragement that Edward decided to turn his hand to verse and as soon as he started writing — using the name "Edward Eastaway" — poems came to him naturally. The long and painful apprenticeship was at last over; he was now a master with words and eager to express exactly what he felt and thought.

In July 1915 the burgeoning poet enlisted in the Artists' Rifles. He had thought long and hard about the war, disliking the patriotic flag-waving and drumbanging, but aware that serving the country he loved — and more specifically the English countryside he loved — was something that he could not turn away from. He could have gone to live in America with Frost, and could, quite easily, have obtained a safe, easy job in the Army. But he didn't. He gained a commission in the Royal Artillery, volunteered for service overseas and after putting his affairs in order, embarked from Southampton in January 1917. He had been writing poetry constantly and plans were going ahead for the publication of a selection of his verse and also for the inclusion of some of his poems in *An Annual of New Poetry* which eventually appeared in the spring of 1917.

Once he was at the Front, he calmly put away all thoughts of home, books and poetry, glad to be doing something useful and active, and greatly liked by the other men who looked upon him as a sort of father figure. On 8th April he was with the guns at Arras when a shell came whizzing over and hit the ground just a yard from where he was standing. It failed to go off. That evening in the mess the other officers pulled his leg about it, saying that a man with his luck would be safe wherever he went. Early next morning Edward was at the observation post when another shell was fired from the German lines. This time he was not so lucky. As the battle raged on, his body was retrieved and he was buried in the military cemetery of Agny.

Unlike most of the other soldier-poets Edward Thomas did not recount the ghastly horrors of the war in his verse. His method was to reflect more quietly, relating it to the ordinary men and women and the English countryside of which he was so fond. A gentle melancholy informs his poems, and works like "As the Team's Head Brass", a simple country conversation, say it all, without ever, as it were, raising their voices.

"If one word could tell of his all," wrote Walter de la Mare, "that word would be England . . . England's roads and heaths and woods, its secret haunts and solitudes, its houses, its people — themselves resembling its thorns and junipers — its very flint and dust, were his freedom and its peace . . . When Edward Thomas was killed a mirror of England was shattered . . ."

STEPHEN GARNETT

A photograph of James Drummond Burns taken shortly after he joined up.

JAMES BURNS

(1895-1915)

A mong the millions of troops who fought and died on the scattered, sprawling battlefields of the First World War, none were more deserving of their high reputation for courage and daring than the dashing soldiers of the Australian and New Zealand Army Corps known as "ANZACS". In 1914, when the call to arms went out from England to the far-flung corners of her Empire, young men from these two nations, feeling a duty and loyalty to their mother country that today would probably be scoffed at as old-fashioned and out of place, volunteered in their thousands.

This powerful sense of comradeship and the sharing of a common cause with England which so many ordinary men felt was captured by one of these Australians, 19-year-old Corporal Jim Burns of the 21st Battalion, AIF, in a dramatic piece of verse entitled "For England", (reproduced later in this chapter). Burns wrote the poem for his school magazine shortly before joining up, and during 1915, when it was widely published in both England and Australia, it played an important part in persuading many other men to enlist.

Tragically, like countless numbers of his contemporaries, young Jim Burns did not live to develop and

An Australian soldier at Gallipoli observes Turkish positions by means of a trench periscope.

enjoy his huge potential, either as a man or as a poet. On 18th September 1915, just 10 days after landing at Gallipoli in the Dardanelles, and only three months after his twentieth birthday, he was shot in the head and killed. All those who had served with him felt the loss keenly, but perhaps the greatest indication of just how much Jim had meant to his family and friends was conveyed in the pages of a little booklet published soon after his death by his old school, Scotch College in a suburb of Melbourne.

Entitled *In the Dawning of the Day*, the book was a touching tribute to Jim Burns, with words of praise from his headmaster and containing several other poems that Jim had written whilst still a much-loved pupil there. The twenty or so pages also included some interesting biographical details about the boy who, during his all too brief life, had enjoyed such a dazzling career.

James Drummond Burns was born on 18th June, 1895, the elder son of the Reverend H. M. Burns of the Presbyterian Manse at Lilydale, a small country town in the state of Victoria. His grandfather, also named James Drummond Burns, (1823-1864), had been a church minister in Hampstead, London, and a talented hymn-writer and poet from whom Jim obviously inherited his literary talent.

Jim was a pupil at Scotch College, the oldest surviving school in Victoria, for four years, during which time he made such an impact that his achievements are still held up as something to which present-day pupils should strive.

Not only was he brilliant academically — winning the school's Shakespeare prize, the exhibition in English, and gaining a first-class honours in History and Latin which won him a scholarship to Ormond College — but he was also an outstanding athlete, rowing for the college eight and representing the school at athletics.

But it was as editor of the school magazine, the *Scotch Collegian* — a post he held for two years — that Jim really made his mark. The high standards of behaviour that he set himself and the lofty ideals that guided his every action shine from the pages of his

For England

The bugles of England
Were blowing o'er the sea,
As they had called a thousand years,
Calling now to me;
They woke me from dreaming
In the dawning of the day,
The bugles of England . . .
And how could I stay?

The banners of England,
Unfurled across the sea,
Floating out upon the wind,
Were beckoning to me;
Storm-rent and battle-torn,
Smoke-stained and grey,
The banners of England . . .
And how could I stay?

O, England, I heard the cry
Of those that died for thee,
Sounding like an organ-voice
Across the winter sea;
They lived and died for England,
And gladly went their way,
England, O England . . .
How *could* I stay?

JAMES DRUMMOND BURNS

A drawing of Scotch College.

editorials. As the following extract from one of these articles illustrates, he was devoted to the college, believing that academic and athletic prowess were only of value if they served to uplift and inspire the school as a whole:

For sixty years, succeeding generations of schoolboys have gone forth as men, with the stamp of the School on their brow, and the love of the School in their hearts. But as these have departed, their places have been filled by eager crowds, to whom all the new and strange experiences present "the glory and the freshness of a dream". And these in their turn become part of the life of that School, which they so soon learn to honour and love, and in their turn, change and pass. But the one remains. Unaffected by time or circumstance, the School stands, a mighty edifice in whose uprearing so many have borne a part. And because some are going who will not return, because the way of many must henceforth lie apart from that of the School, there is nothing to regret and nothing to fear. But there is much to remember and much to hope. Each has given something, not much, perhaps, but "some fragment from his dream of human life", which has become a part of the School, and which shall share in her glory and stand with her as an everlasting monument. And in return, how much each has gained! How the memories of these happy days, stored in the inner chambers of the mind, will troop forth at some far-distant time, to brighten dark days when the glory of the dream of life seems faded and worthless! It is these memories and this spirit of loyalty and devotion which will remain long after all other lessons have been forgotten, to remind us for ever of that School whose love will never fade from our hearts, whose glory will never be dimmed in our eyes.

As well as fine prose pieces like this, which seemed to promise so much for the future, the magazine also provided a platform on which Jim could display his poetic talents. And his verse, too, suggested that he would one day become a major literary figure.

Australian recruitment poster.

From Jim's love of the school and all that it represented branched that wider loyalty and devotion to the country and Empire which, at the beginning of 1915, led him to volunteer for active service.

He joined his battalion at Broadmeadows, Victoria, in February and they set sail for Egypt on May 8th. It was at the end of August that they left Cairo on board the *Southland*, for the ill-fated landing at Gallipoli on September 10th. Just over a week later Jim Burns was dead, killed by a bullet from a Turkish rifle.

Tributes to the young poet were swift in coming, with many moving words from those soldiers who had served with him illustrating how Jim Burns had taken into the army all the impressive qualities that he had displayed at Scotch College. Just as he had done during his days as a pupil, he influenced for the better everyone whose life he touched. The army chaplain recalled how he always used to look for Jim's "serious face and great beautiful eyes" at their Communion services in the trenches, which Jim usually persuaded the rest of the soldiers in his tent to attend. And the pages

The Gentle Lady

The gentle lady comes to me
When all the lights are dim,
When o'er the shadowy hill appears
The big moon's yellow rim,
When beetles flit and shrilly sounds
The cricket's evening hymn.

O gentle lady, come tonight,
The earth is rapt and still;
The stars are leaning from the sky
Upon the earth, until
They seem to whisper tender dreams
To sleeping plain and hill.

JAMES DRUMMOND BURNS

of *In the Dawning of the Day* contained a further enlightening insight into the character of this gifted young man, written by Jim's successor as editor of the school magazine in December 1915:

> He had a singularly charming and attractive personality. His quiet dignity, his kindly sympathy, his keen sense of humour, endeared him to a host of friends. Concerning his own attainments he was unassumingly modest; over the success of a friend he was tremendously enthusiastic. He was a keen observer and an excellent judge of character. His wide reading and his clear and philosophical mind made him a most interesting and instructive conversationalist. In temperament he was remarkably cool and self-controlled. He had a high sense of honour. Few came into contact with him who did not feel the influence of his noble character.

And there were also these words from W.S. Littlejohn, the headmaster of Scotch College . . .

> His was a rare combination of gifts of heart and head and hand, and he brought them all to the service of his school. And his richest bequest was one he was quite unconscious of bestowing — the influence of a strong manly character. He cherished the highest ideals of life. Whatsoever things were pure and honourable, and just and lovable and gracious, he thought on these things, and left behind the fragrance of a consecrated life . . .
>
> We had visions for him of a brilliant future, a time when his pen would be an inspiration to a young country struggling into nationhood. But it was not to be, for he was called to the higher service. He gave his life for us, and the school will not forget.

Thanks to the power of his poem "For England" — an unashamedly patriotic piece of verse written by a

The school's Memorial Hall where the names of all those former pupils who fell in the First World War are listed.

young man who never even set foot in England — no-one who loves this country, her character, her history and her traditions, and believes they are worth fighting for, will ever forget Jim Burns or his stirring words . . .   STEPHEN GARNETT

To the Dead

Since in the days that may not come again
The sun has shone for us on English fields,
Since we have marked the years with thanksgiving,
Nor been ungrateful for the loveliness
Which is our England, then tho' we walk no more
The woods together, lie in the grass no more,
For us the long grass blows, the woods are green,
For us the valleys smile, the streams are bright,
For us the kind sun still is comfortable
And the birds sing; and since your feet and mine
Have trod the lanes together, climbed the hills,
Then in the lanes and on the little hills
Our feet are beautiful for evermore.
And you — O if I call you, you will come
Most loved, most lovely faces of my friends
Who are so safely housed within my heart,
So parcel of this blessed spirit land
Which in my own heart is England, so possessed
Of all its ways to walk familiarly
And be at home, that I can count on you,
Loving you so, being loved, to wait for me,
So may I turn me in and by some sweet
Remembered pathway find you once again.
Then we can walk together, I with you,
Or you, or you, along some quiet road,
And talk the foolish, old, forgivable talk,
And laugh together; you will turn your head,
Look as you used to look, speak as you spoke,
My friend to me, and I your friend to you.
Only when at the last, by some cross-road,
Our longer shadows, falling on the grass,

Turn us back homeward, and the setting sun
Shines like a golden glory round your head,
There will be something sudden and strange in you.
Then you will lean and look into my eyes,
And I shall see the bright wound at your side,
And feel the new blood flowing to my heart,
Your blood, beloved, flowing to my heart,
And I shall hear you speaking in my ear —
O not the old, forgivable, foolish talk,
But flames and exaltations, and desires,
But hopes, and comprehensions, and resolves,
But holy, incommunicable things,
That like immortal birds sing in my breast,
And springing from a fire of sacrifice,
Beat with bright wings about the throne of God.

GERALD CALDWELL SIORDET

A Sussex Lane

This poem first appeared under the title "Chance Memory" in the *Daily News*, June, 1916, at the height of the Great War.

I can't forget the lane that goes from Steyning to the Ring
In Summertime, and on the Down, how larks and linnets sing
High in the sun. The wind comes off the sea, and oh, the air!
I never knew till now that life in old days was so fair.
But now I know it in this filthy rat-infested ditch,
When every shell must kill or spare, and God alone knows which,
And I am made a beast of prey, and this trench is my lair —
My God! I never knew till now that those days were so fair.
And we assault in half an hour, and — it's a silly thing —
I can't forget the lane that goes from Steyning to the Ring.

PHILIP JOHNSON

John Magee, "The Pilot Poet", in the uniform of the RCAF.

JOHN MAGEE

(1922-1941)

I t was a grey, overcast day in December 1941, and in the skies above the flat Fenland countryside of south Lincolnshire a squadron of Spitfires was returning home to its base near the village of Wellingore after an uneventful morning patrol. The young pilot of one of the aeroplanes was a handsome 19-year-old called John Magee. As he looked down on the vast patchwork of fields, criss-crossed by long straight lanes and dotted here and there with farms and cottages, the feeling of exhilaration that he felt whenever he took to the air again swept over him.

Soaring above the matchstick-sized figures far below, John wouldn't have changed places with anyone. The Spitfire had proved itself to be the swiftest and most deadly fighter plane in the skies, and as he sat at the controls of his own machine with every sense and sinew perfectly tuned to the feel of its fabric around him, and the familiar sound of its engine, John felt as free as a bird. He was a knight of the skies riding a charger that would respond like lightning to his every command; and, if he came under attack from any enemy aircraft, twist and turn out of the way with awe-inspiring speed.

Were it not for the presence of his fellow-flyers and

the need to be in a constant state of readiness for the call to intercept enemy bombers coming in from the North Sea, John would probably have opened up the throttle and put the Spitfire through its paces, for to soar and swoop through the heavens was the supreme experience of his life. This love of flying was coupled with an equally powerful passion for writing poetry — the spiralling freedom of flight finding softer, more subtle echoes in the dramatic rising and falling of poetic rhythms.

In fact, when it came to poetry, John Magee was a genius. He had demonstrated this a few months earlier after his very first flight in command of a Spitfire, when his two great gifts for poetry and flying had come rapturously together to create *High Flight* (see overleaf), a poem which has in the past 50 years become a rousing anthem for pilots everywhere. It has been reproduced in scores of anthologies and now hangs on the walls at air training schools and flying museums throughout England, Canada and the USA.

But this was all in the future, and as he started his descent to the airfield at Wellingore, which was suddenly obscured by a thick bank of cloud, John could have had no idea of just how famous *High Flight* would become — he had only ever shown it to his family and a few close friends. Nevertheless, no-one who knew John Magee would have been surprised that his poetic genius had flowered so quickly. He had lived his short life at full speed, an unusual background of wide travel and hard-fought personal battles giving him experience and maturity far beyond his years. As the aeroplane disappeared into the clouds on that day in 1941, it was only John's dogged determination and burning desire to assist in the defence of England that meant he was there at all. Had he listened to the advice

The site of RAF Wellingore as it looks today, nearly 50 years after John's final flight.

of others and put aside his own feelings and beliefs in favour of a safer existence, his life story, which as we shall see had an untimely and tragic conclusion, might have been completely different . . .

John Gillespie Magee was born on 9th June, 1922, thousands of miles away from the England that he came to love, in the busy Chinese port of Shanghai. His parents were a remarkable couple: his father, John Magee senior, an American who had turned his back on a life of wealth, influence and opportunity in Pittsburgh to become a priest of the Episcopal Church and a missionary in China; his mother, Faith Emmeline Backhouse, a genteel English lady from Helmingham in Suffolk who had gone to China as a member of the Church Missionary Society — a daring and highly unconventional step for an unmarried English lady in those days. As both were missionaries working in Nanking it was inevitable that they would

(Continued on page 225)

221

HIGH FLIGHT

by John Magee

Oh! I have slipped the surly bonds of Earth
And danced the skies
        on laughter-silvered wings;
Sunward I've climbed,
        and joined the tumbling mirth
Of sun-split clouds
        — and done a hundred things
You have not dreamed of —
        wheeled and soared and swung
High in the sunlit silence.
        Hov'ring there,
I've chased the shouting wind along,
        and flung
My eager craft through footless
        halls of air. . .
Up, up the long, delirious burning blue
I've topped the wind-swept heights
        with easy grace,
Where never lark,
        or even eagle flew —
And, while with silent, lifting mind
        I've trod
The high untrespassed sanctity of space,
Put out my hand and touched the face of God.

Some present-day pupils enjoy a game of cricket at Rugby School.

(Continued from page 221)

be drawn into one another's company. Eventually, on 19th July, 1921, they were married.

The couple were both very proud of their origins and keen that their sons should also have knowledge of their Anglo-American roots — John was the eldest, but there would be four boys in all: David Backhouse (6th July, 1925), Christopher Walford (19th August, 1928) and Frederick Hugh (23rd August, 1933). They planned, therefore, when the boys were old enough, to send them first to school in England and then to college in the USA. Before that, John started his education at the American School in Nanking, speaking English while he was there and then reverting to the Chinese tongue when he returned to the mission compound in the evening.

In November 1931, when John was nine, as the first part of his "English" education he was sent to St. Clare's boarding school near Walmer in Kent — travelling by boat in the company of his mother and two younger brothers who were going to stay at Grandmother Backhouse's home in Kent. John quickly made an impression at St. Clare's. Scholastically he was far above average and, with confidence and experience unusual for one so young, rebelled against the tedium of routine and was always quick to join in any mischief.

In 1935 when he was 13 his parents moved him to Rugby's famous public school in Warwickshire — a venerable English institution steeped in history and tradition. Trevor Hoy, John's room-mate at Rugby from 1935 to 1939, with whom he shared a tiny, closet-like study, remembers him as "an audacious rule-breaker and pioneer" following in the footsteps, in many respects, of William Webb Ellis whose

225

The boys of School House in 1936. John Magee is fifth from the left in the front row.

exploits are commemorated on a plaque in the school's famous Close. He it was who, in 1823, "with a fine disregard for the rules of football as played in his time, first took the ball in his arms and ran with it, thus originating the distinctive feature of the Rugby game".

But John's greatest hero among the many famous Rugby old boys was the war poet Rupert Brooke (1887-1915), featured in another chapter of this book.

John's own attempts at writing verse were arousing favourable comment amongst his teachers, particularly from the headmaster, P.H.B. (Hugh) Lyon, who was himself a gifted poet with several books of verse to his credit. John became a close friend of the Lyon family and was one of several schoolboys who accompanied them on picnics and holidays in Yorkshire and the Lake District. At this time, John fell hopelessly in love with Elinor, the headmaster's eldest daughter, who was a year older than himself.

*The Lyon family and friends on holiday in the Lake District in 1937.
John Magee is on the right of the picture next to the headmaster,
Elinor is in the centre.*

Described by his housemaster as "intelligent, volatile, emotional, untidy, thoughtless, keen", John enjoyed life to the full at Rugby, playing football and tennis, taking part in rifle-practice, and during the holidays sailing his own dinghy in the Channel. He did well in his studies but was still inclined to throw himself into wild pranks, like the time he climbed onto the roof of the School House and tied a label with his name on it to the hand of the clock!

As news filtered over to England from Europe, and the possibility of another war loomed larger and larger, they were difficult times for the boys, uncertain as to what their futures would be. John would never accept anything without first questioning it, and having grown up just after what was supposed to have

John, aged 16, showing his mother the letter informing him that he has won the school's Poetry Prize.

been "the war to end all wars", and with first-hand experience of warfare from his childhood in China, in the uncertain atmosphere of 1939 his thoughts turned towards pacifism and doubts about conventional religion. This frame of mind was revealed in his poem *Brave New World* with which he won the coveted Rugby Poetry Prize. His hero, Rupert Brooke, on whose work he based many of his own creations, had won the same school prize in 1905.

In the summer of 1939, so that he could complete his education and also get to know something of his American roots, John was persuaded somewhat against his wishes to go to America and stay with his aunt in Pittsburgh, Pennsylvania. He attended the Avon School near Hartford, Connecticut, where he quickly impressed one of his teachers as "the most intelligent person who has ever come to the school". Despite a busy social life and dates with a constantly changing stream of pretty girls, John wasn't very happy at Avon, largely because, with England now at war and in dire peril, he felt out of it and anxious to play a part himself.

"I shall never be really happy over here", he wrote to Hugh Lyon. "Don't you believe a man should live by his convictions? I am convinced my place is in England and, if ever I see the opportunity, I'm coming".

Whilst he was at Avon, John worked in the school printing shop and produced an attractive little volume containing 17 of his poems. Copies were circulated privately to his family and friends, but it was never made available to the public. The high quality of the poems showed what a remarkable 17-year-old John Magee was, but despite the satisfaction that seeing his poems in print undoubtedly brought him, by the spring of 1940 he was becoming increasingly restless.

MORTALITY

WHO can forget white lilies in the spring,
The agony of poppies, stabbing corn?
— Do you remember once when I was king,
And you my queen, how on the perfect lawn
We ruled the daisies while we laughed at play?
... And I must live, to see the colours start
To life; when all the world is young in May,
And honeysuckle rushes to the heart ...

I will not die, while roses laugh in June,
When Beauty wanders through slow, secret ways,
And sombre winter leaps again to mirth ...
Oh! Death comes swift and cold, and all too soon —
And I must live, while sleepy summer days,
And You — and You — are lovely on the earth!

JOHN MAGEE

Not only did he find it impossible to concentrate on anything else when England was under such a threat, but he was scared that his enthusiasm and creativity were dying within him. He felt too safe and comfortable and needed a challenge so that he could prove himself.

Mr. and Mrs. Magee planned to send him to Yale in the autumn of 1940 but, as the Battle of Britain raged thoughout the summer, despite the fact that he had

John receiving his "Wings" from his Station Commander in June 1941.

won the top classical scholarship John's determination to join up became irresistible. After a long discussion it was finally decided to let him have his way, and he joined the Royal Canadian Air Force. Mr. Magee was now the assistant rector of a church in Washington, so John was able to punctuate his training with periods of home leave. Air Force discipline had turned him into an assured and purposeful young man, even if he was still something of a dare-devil who delighted in risky aerobatics.

John received his all-important "Wings" in June 1941 and shortly afterwards was posted to Great Britain and his final training station at Llandow in South Wales. On one of his days off he flew to Kemerton in Gloucestershire where his first love, Elinor, and the rest of the Lyon family were staying with friends for the fruit-picking season. John terrified the sleepy little

232

village as he buzzed low over the house before landing in a field!

It was while he was in the officers' mess one day at Llandow, talking in a loud, excited voice about the qualities of the Spitfire, that a fellow-flyer suggested to him that as he was interested in writing poetry, he ought to put his feelings down in words. Immediately John took an envelope from his pocket and in no time at all he had scribbled down the words of what was to become the most famous flying poem in the world, *High Flight*. Soon after, when he had completed his final training and joined 412 Squadron at RAF Digby in Lincolnshire, he sent a copy of the verse to his parents.

John joined the all-Canadian 412 Squadron at RAF Digby in September 1941, having received a glowing assessment report from his squadron commander at Llandow. Time was divided between practising man-oeuvres, taking part in usually uneventful coastal patrols, attacking shipping or intercepting bombers over the North Sea and Holland, and enduring that curse of all fighter pilots during the last war, the nail-biting wait for a call to action. There were also, of course, the parties in the mess that followed any particularly dangerous or successful exercise. On these occasions, John and the other young flyers would unwind as only fighter pilots knew how. John was a very popular member of the squadron and there was a great sense of comradeship amongst them all.

At the end of October on seven days' leave he visited Oxford where Elinor was a student at Lady Margaret Hall; John was quite sure that he was in love with her. Elinor, who now lives on the coast of Wales, vividly remembered the meeting:

"Before he went back to the squadron he came to

John Magee (on the right) with one of his fellow-flyers at their aerodrome in Lincolnshire shortly before his death.

say good-bye and brought an old motor-bicycle he had acquired. It was just like him, I thought, to buy a cycle that kept breaking down and had to be pushed most of the time, and it caused him great amusement by its eccentricities. We shook hands rather solemnly when he went and it seemed rather foolish and inadequate to wish him good luck, because whatever happened he considered himself marvellously lucky and I never remember him complaining of anything. The motor-bike, however, cheered us up a bit; it went five yards and then stopped dead, and when at last it went on again we laughed and John waved his hand and disappeared round the corner."

John sent his family another poem, *Per Ardua* (the motto of the Royal Canadian Air Force was "Per Ardua Ad Astra"), and wrote the following dedication and verses:

To those who gave their lives to England during the Battle of Britain and left such a shining example to us who follow, these lines are dedicated.

PER ARDUA

They that have climbed the white mists of the morning,
They that have soared before the world's awake,
To herald up their foemen to them, scorning
The thin dawn's rest their weary folk might take.

Some that have left other mouths to tell the story
Of high, blue battle, quite young limbs that bled;
How they had thundered up the clouds to glory,
Or fallen to an English field stained red.

Because my faltering feet would fail I find them
Laughing beside me, steadying the hand
That seeks their deadly courage — yet behind them
The cold light dies in that once brilliant land . . .

Do these, who help the quickened pulse run slowly,
Whose stern, remembered image cools the brow,
Till the far dawn of Victory, know only
Night's darkness, and Valhalla's silence now?

John's flying ability improved all the time and he was soon a section leader, taking part in operations over occupied Europe. So it was that he came to be flying towards Wellingore on that December day in 1941.

While undergoing his fighter training John had once written: "I want to die in circumstances violently heroic", but as he descended through that bank of cloud, suddenly the unthinkable happened — he collided with another aircraft from the nearby RAF College at Cranwell. A farmer working near the village of Roxholm witnessed the incident. Looking up, he actually saw John climb out of his doomed aircraft in an attempt to use his parachute. In the event, it got tangled up and failed to open. Both young men were killed.

John was buried in the village cemetery at Scopwick in Lincolnshire, close to where he died and alongside many of his friends who had also been killed defending Britain. The headstone of his grave bears the first and last lines of *High Flight*.

John's death came as a great shock to Elinor. "He liked to live life at full speed", she wrote, "and danger only made life more thrilling. I don't think he could have borne to grow old."

At the time of his death *High Flight* was virtually unknown, but after John's father had it printed in his

Flowers adorn John's grave in the little village cemetery at Scopwick.

church magazine it was spotted by a reporter and published in a Washington newspaper, when it captured the imaginations of the thousands who read it. More recently the poem was referred to by President Reagan in his speech to the American people following the "Challenger" disaster in January 1986.

So, through this great work, the memory and spirit of John Magee lives on . . . nearly 50 years after he himself "touched the face of God".

STEPHEN GARNETT

BIBLIOGRAPHY

Background Reading and Anthologies

The English Poets of the First World War by John Lehmann (Thames and Hudson, 1981); *The Oxford Book of War Poetry* (Oxford University Press, 1984); *In Time of War* (Blackie and Son, 1987); *The Pity of War* (Shepheard-Walwyn, 1985); *Verse of Valour* (Art and Educational Publishers, 1943).

The Poets

Rupert Brooke: *Rupert Brooke: His Life and Legend* by John Lehmann (Weidenfeld and Nicolson, 1980); *Poetical Works* (Faber and Faber, 1974).

Keith Douglas: *Keith Douglas 1920-44* by Desmond Graham (Oxford University Press, 1974); *The Complete Poems of Keith Douglas* (Oxford University Press, 1978).

James Farrar: *The Unreturning Spring* (Chatto and Windus, 1950).

Ivor Gurney: *The Ordeal of Ivor Gurney* by Michael Hurd (Oxford University Press, 1978); *Stars in a Dark Night: The Letters of Ivor Gurney to the Chapman Family* by Anthony Boden (Alan Sutton, 1986); *Collected Poems of Ivor Gurney* edited by P.J. Kavanagh (Oxford University Press, 1982).

F.W. Harvey: *F.W. Harvey: Soldier, Poet* by Anthony Boden (Alan Sutton, 1988); *Gloucestershire Friends* (Sidgwick and Jackson, 1917).

Noel Hodgson: *Verse and Prose in Peace and War* (Smith, Elder and Co., 1916); *The New Elizabethans* by E.B. Osborn (Bodley Head, 1919); *The Devonshire Regiment 1914-1918* by C.T. Atkinson.

Geoffrey Studdert Kennedy: *Woodbine Willie* by William Purcell (Mowbray, 1962); *The Unutterable Beauty* (Hodder and Stoughton, 1938).

John Magee: *Sunward I've Climbed* by Herman Hagedorn (Macmillan, New York, 1942); *The Complete Works of John Magee: The Pilot Poet* (This England Books, 1989).

Wilfred Owen: *Wilfred Owen* by Jon Stallworthy (Oxford University Press, 1974); *Collected Poems* (Chatto and Windus, 1963).

Ernest Raymond: *The Story of My Days: An Autobiography 1888-1922* (Cassell, 1968); *Please You, Draw Near: An Autobiography 1922-1968* (Cassell, 1969).

Vivian Rosewarne: The information is taken from an article on Rosewarne by Christopher Elliott which appeared in the Winter 1988 edition of *This England*.

Siegfried Sassoon: *Siegfried's Journey* (Faber and Faber, 1945); *Collected Poems* (Faber and Faber, 1947).

Charles Sorley: *Charles Hamilton Sorley: A Biography* by Jean Moorcroft Wilson (Cecil Woolf, 1985); *The Collected Poems of Charles Hamilton Sorley* (Cecil Woolf, 1985).

Edward Thomas: *Edward Thomas: A Poet for his Country* by Jan Marsh (Elek Books, 1978); *Collected Poems* (Oxford University Press, 1981).

PHOTOGRAPHS

Front Cover: Bill Meadows; Alan Hutchinson, pages 26, 84, 180, 200; Geoffrey Wright, page 44; Gerald Pillow, page 57; E. Emrys Jones, pages 80, 146; Arthur Cook, page 83; Clifford Robinson, page 104; T.H. Williams, page 117; John Tarlton, pages 126, 153; Vernon Shaw, page 139; A. Sinclair, page 177; William Law, page 189; Back Cover: Michael Oldfield.

This England